THIS IS BIGGER

This Is Bigger

How Community, Calling, and Courage Create Impact

Stacey Collins

Published by Game Changer Publishing

Paperback ISBN: 979-8-90158-101-8

Hardcover ISBN: 979-8-90158-090-5

Digital ISBN: 979-8-90158-096-7

www.GameChangerPublishing.com

ADVANCE PRAISE

"Stacey Collins is as real as they come, both in person and online. Supportive, inspiring, and funny in the best way, she brings joy to everyone she meets. This book captures her heart for community, her journey of faith, and the story behind the business she's built. From laughter to tears, you'll feel every emotion reading these pages. Whether you're a fellow content creator or someone who craves meaningful community, there's something in this book that you'll connect to."

—Kristy Bottle, Owner of Kristy's Craft Room

"Stacey Collins journey had me in tears, gave me chills, and made me laugh. She gives a wonderful example of going all in and trusting God with bold dreams! This book will inspire you to see things from a bigger perspective and reimagine your own purpose!"

—Danielle Stringer Founder of Imperfect Dust and Author of The Maker's Guide to Multiplying

"*This Is Bigger* beautifully captures what happens when faith, courage, and community come together. Watching Stacey build Wilshire Collections has been truly inspiring, but reading the deeper "why" behind it all is incredibly powerful. If you're searching for inspiration, clarity, or the courage to take your next step, her book will remind you that you're not alone, your calling matters, and what God is doing through you is bigger than you think."

—Blair Moore, Founder of BeStyled Co.

"This book is a beautiful, powerful testimony of resilience, faith, and straight-up grit from start to finish. What I love most is how Stacey shares all of her journey, not just the polished, highlight-reel moments. She reminds us that humble beginnings, hard seasons, and a few bumps and bruises along the way don't disqualify us... they shape us. Through consistency, listening to your heart, staying connected to your community, and serving with everything you have, something truly special can be built, often more beautiful than you ever imagined. Her humor and genuine spirit shine on every page, leaving you feeling encouraged, seen, and fully capable of going after what God has placed on your heart. I'm incredibly grateful that our businesses crossed paths, and even more grateful to now call her a true friend."

—Brooke Riley, Owner and Founder of
Re-Fabbed and Re-Fabbed Boutique

TO MY HUSBAND AND MY BOYS

Anthony

Thank you for your constant encouragement and support of my dreams, for the laughs when I needed them most, for being the calm to my storm, for listening to every crazy idea and never making me feel crazy, and for believing in me long before I believed in myself. You've loved me through every chapter of this journey, and there's no one I would rather do this life with. I'll never be able to thank you enough for being the amazing husband, father, and constant support that you are! I love you so much!

Parker and Tyler

You've been by my side since you were little, watching this business grow. I hope it has encouraged you to dream big, work hard, chase your passions, and live out your calling. Thank you for embracing this "crazy job" of mine and for your love, support, and protectiveness along the way. You are the reason I work hard, but also the reason I slow down to soak it all up. I love you both so much, and I hope you know that being your mom is the best job I've ever had and ever will have. It is a true gift!

You three are my world, my joy, and my greatest blessings in life. This book is for all of you.

READ THIS FIRST

Just to say thanks for buying and reading my book, I would
like to give you a free printable + some other fun ideas and inspiration
+ share ways you can get connected with the Wilshire Community!
Thank you!

Stacey

Scan the QR Code now to get yours:

THIS IS BIGGER

HOW COMMUNITY, CALLING, AND COURAGE
CREATE IMPACT

STACEY COLLINS

FOREWORD

Some people build businesses.

Others build communities.

And then there are rare people like Stacey Collins, who may start with paintbrushes, pillows, or printables, but what they are really building is connection.

There is something deeply human about wanting to belong, to feel connected to something meaningful, especially in seasons where life feels heavy, quiet, or isolating. So many women carry their creativity, their questions, and their longing for connection silently, unsure if there is a place where they truly fit. Unsure if what they love, what they are drawn to, or who they are really matters.

This book meets you right there.

I first met Stacey in 2020. I had known of her for a little while before that, but getting to know her personally was something different entirely. Even then, she had a growing audience and a clear creative voice, but what stood out to me immediately was how grounded she was. There was no performance. No pretense. Just Stacey—fun, kind, wildly creative, and exactly who she appeared to be.

There was never a sense that she was trying to impress anyone or be someone she was not. What you saw on the screen was exactly who she was behind the scenes. That consistency, between who she is publicly and who she is privately, is rare. And it is one of the reasons people do not just follow Stacey. They trust her. They feel safe with her.

If you have ever watched her "whisper shop," you know exactly what I mean.

Over time, our relationship deepened. What began as a coaching relationship quickly grew into a friendship. I have had the privilege of being Stacey's coach, mentor, and someone who has had a front-row seat to her journey, not just the wins you see online, but the questions, the hesitations, and the moments where she wondered if she should stay small and safe.

And that is where this title comes from.

When you are inside your own work, it is often impossible to see it clearly. Creatives, especially those with servant hearts, tend to minimize what comes naturally to them. They focus on what they have not done yet instead of recognizing what is already changing lives. They downplay the impact because it feels normal to them. Easy. Familiar.

Stacey was no different.

She was so focused on serving her community well that she had not fully paused to recognize just how much space she already held in their lives. How deeply women connected to her voice, her creativity, and her presence. How what she had built went far beyond projects or products.

The moment that stands out most for me was when Stacey brought up the idea of having her pillows designed and manufactured. On the surface, it sounded like a product decision. But I knew instantly this was bigger than selling pillows.

This was about creating something tangible, something her community could bring into their homes, sit with, live with, and feel connected to. A piece of Stacey, wrapped in creativity and care, that would live on couches and chairs long after a Facebook Live ended.

What she was really offering went far beyond decor. A way for her community to feel connected to her creativity month after month, in a way that was personal and lasting. That kind of connection does not come from products alone. It comes from trust. From consistency. From showing up genuinely, over and over again. And Stacey had been quietly building that for years.

She did not see it that way at first. Stacey has a tendency to underestimate just how deeply people connect with her work. I say that with a smile because if you know her, you know it is true. She wanted to play it safe. She wanted to keep things manageable. But sometimes, part of my job as a coach is to lovingly stretch someone beyond what feels comfortable and help them see what is possible.

This was one of those moments.

What Stacey has built is not accidental. It is the result of showing up consistently, honestly, and generously, even when it felt scary. It is the result of creating spaces where people feel welcome, seen, and invited to be part of something together. And that is exactly what you will find in these pages.

This book is for you.

For the hobbyist.

For the decorator.

For the woman who tunes in just to hear Stacey's big, bold voice and feel a little less alone.

It is for the moments you have questioned whether what you love really matters and for the seasons when you have felt disconnected or unsure of what comes next.

You do not need to consider yourself creative, and you do not need to have everything figured out. You simply need to be open to the idea that being part of something meaningful can change how you see yourself and what feels possible.

As you read, I hope you do not just see Stacey's story. I hope you see yourself reflected in it. I hope you recognize the beauty of community, the power of showing up as you are, and the comfort of knowing you do not have to do life alone. Because the truth is, this really is bigger.

Bigger than one woman.

Bigger than one business.

Bigger than any single moment.

Belonging has a ripple effect. When women feel seen, they show up differently. When they feel encouraged, they create more freely. When they know they are not alone, they take braver steps, sometimes without even realizing it.

And by picking up this book, you are already a part of it.

— **Sarah Williams**, Founder of *Launch Your Box* & Best-selling author of *One Box At A Time*

CONTENTS

INTRODUCTION

I'm a Southern girl, born and raised in Nashville, Tennessee. I'm a child of God, wife, mom, daughter, friend, and business owner. Thirteen-plus years ago, I was all of those except the business owner.

Before I became a mom, I worked in pharmaceutical sales. At the time, that felt like a dream job to me. While the pay was good and the perks were even better, I realize now that it was not fulfilling to me at all.

My entire sales team was let go on the due date of my firstborn son. At the time, I thought it was absolutely devastating. My husband and I had no idea what we were going to do, especially since I had planned to return to work after my maternity leave. Looking back now, I see what a blessing that moment truly was.

We made the decision that I would stay home and spend those early years with our son. Those years were incredibly special.

Later, when we were trying to have our second child, we faced a long struggle with infertility. During that time, I decided to take a part-time pharmaceutical job. It allowed me to be home with my oldest while also contributing to our family and giving me a much-needed outlet during a difficult season.

A couple of years into that job, guess what happened?

My entire sales team was laid off again. Once again, I was crushed and unsure of what I would do next. But right in the middle of job searching, we found out we were pregnant with our second son after two and a half years of trying.

My husband and I decided once again to view this as a blessing in disguise. I would stay home with him during those early years, too. Being a stay-at-home mom is, without a doubt, the hardest yet most fulfilling job I've ever had, and likely ever will have. I wouldn't trade those years for the world. Still, deep down, I always felt there was more waiting for me.

At the time, I didn't know what that "more" was. My youngest was eighteen months old, my oldest was in second grade, and I was struggling to find part-time work that would let me stay home while also justifying the cost of childcare. And then, it happened.

Wilshire Collections was born.

I decided that if I couldn't find the right job for myself, I would create one. You'll read all about how that journey started soon, but for now, just know this: I could have never imagined what was about to unfold.

That girl who was laid off twice was stepping into a journey no one could have prepared her for. This book is the result of thirteen-plus years of hard work growing Wilshire Collections, and writing it has been a dream of mine for many of those years. But this book isn't just about me.

Yes, it's about my journey and the community that's grown with me. But more than that, it's about the One who carved the path and guided me every step of the way. And that's what I hope you see over and over again in these pages: a girl with a paintbrush and a dream and a God who paints the most beautiful pictures.

This is Bigger is a story of impact. It's a story of lessons learned, of highs and lows, of choosing faith over fear. It's filled with laughter, and possibly a few tears.

It's a story straight from my heart, one that is so special to me, and I hope it becomes special to you, too. It's written for, and in honor of, my incredible community. But truly, it's for any woman who's ever longed to feel connected, who's ever craved friendship, laughter, prayer, and belonging. This book will show you how those things can show up in the most unexpected ways and places if your heart is open to them.

Maybe you've followed along on my journey, or maybe you picked up this book wondering who in the world this person is. I'm Stacey, the girl behind the dream turned reality. I don't have all the answers, and my story is still being written. But I have a lot to share, and I'm so glad you're here.

Before we dive in, I want you to know this: This book is not just about what happened to me; it's about what's possible for you. It's about what can happen when you step out in faith, when you listen to the quiet nudges, and when you follow the crazy ideas that keep you up at night.

My journey may look different from yours, but I believe God is writing something beautiful in your life, too. And maybe, just maybe, these pages will encourage you to trust Him with your next step.

I hope that the more you read this book, the more you see the story of God using Wilshire to grow this community, the less you see of me. Because this book truly isn't just about me or my story. I hope it makes you smile, laugh, feel those tugs at your heartstrings, and everything in between. I also hope you find deep joy.

CHAPTER 1
FINDING JOY IN THE JOURNEY

I never thought a paintbrush would change my life. Back in 2013, I had no idea that a little hobby would grow into something so much bigger.

I'll never forget the day it happened, the day everything changed for me and opened my eyes to what was really happening. It was 2018, and I was doing what I always did: sharing my love for creating and decorating on social media, hoping to stop someone's scroll and inspire them.

And then one day, I opened my inbox. There it was, a message from a woman named Missy S., someone I had never met, but who was part of my online community. As I started reading, my eyes filled with tears.

Here's what Missy wrote:

> *I just wanted to say thank you, Stacey, for helping me find my joy again. Six years ago, I had a stroke.*
> *They found a tumor, and I was diagnosed with a meningioma brain tumor. I had brain surgery, which left me partially deaf and*

1

double-sighted for a year. Although my deafness is permanent, I regained my sight thanks to vestibular therapy.

They say that after tragedy hits, your faith is tested, and I was tested beyond my limits. I remained true to my words and praised God for letting me live. After my surgery, I went into a deep depression for about two years and couldn't seem to get out of it.

My joy was gone. I really don't know why I'm even writing to you or if you will even read this, but it's important. It's important that you know how you've helped me.

I've been very complacent, silently praying and sitting here at home, doing nothing I truly enjoyed before, until I found you, followed you, and joined your decorating group. Since then, I've painted the inside of my home and started decorating again, and I've felt joy coming back into my life. I'm usually a silent, shy person, but you are truly an inspiration to me and have helped me so much.

I can't wait to get my tree decorated and all my stuff out for Christmas because of you. Thank you.
Missy S.

Wow. I must have read those words a dozen times.

They hit me like a ton of bricks. What did she mean that I helped her with something more than decorating? I immediately sent her some video messages back, telling her how much the words meant to me and how thrilled I was to be even a small help to her in such a dark time.

I will never forget this message or the story of Missy. The word *"joy"* became an instant favorite of mine because of that message, and it is now at the heart of everything I do at Wilshire. That message was the moment everything shifted for me.

This wasn't just about decorating or crafting. It wasn't about likes, followers, or even business.

This was about God using the simple to do something extraordinary.

This was about hope in someone's darkest season. This was about connection.

This was the moment I realized that *this is bigger*. Of course, I didn't know any of this back in 2013 when I first dipped my toes into this little business. Back then, it was just me and a paintbrush out in my garage, with a dream that felt more like a hobby than a calling.

I couldn't see the bigger picture yet. I was just creating, sharing, and figuring things out one project at a time. Looking back now, I can see God was laying the foundation all along, even when I didn't understand it.

I honestly never set out to build a big business. I didn't start with wanting to grow a large community or lead a team. I started because I craved a creative outlet in the midst of being a stay-at-home mom to my then-almost two- and seven-year-old boys.

In the struggle to find a part-time job that would allow me to stay with my boys, I found a hobby that I loved. I had always been creative, puff-painting my T-shirts and sponge-painting my bedroom walls. My freshman year of college, I was the only person I knew who hung wallpaper border on the cement walls of my dorm room. Yet I never set out to turn my creative side into any type of business.

I was a mass communications major and a writing minor, and I had held various sales jobs after college before becoming a stay-at-home mom. Then it happened. In November of 2012, that paintbrush I mentioned and a little jar of chalk paint changed my life.

My sister Blair and I picked up our first jar of chalk paint at a holiday market to give it a try. I came home, grabbed a paintbrush, and painted my first piece of furniture, a small end table that I still have to this day. I was hooked.

My sister did the same, and she fell in love with it too. I would literally walk around my house with a paintbrush, trying to figure out what I could paint next. Nothing was safe. I was painting candlesticks, picture frames, old lamps, and more, giving them new life. I became obsessed with all things upcycling and painting.

I'll never forget sitting on the floor of my old bedroom at my parents' house with Blair on Christmas Day 2012. We were both sitting cross-legged on the floor, chatting about life while surrounded by wrapping paper and dreams. Blair and I were talking about this newfound love of chalk paint and painted furniture and how friends and family were already asking us to paint things for them.

That's when we said it out loud: what if we made this a business? We were both at points in our lives when we needed and wanted a change. That dream was laid on our hearts on that Christmas Day, and I can still remember our excitement as we rushed downstairs to tell everyone we were going to start a business.

Did they think we were crazy? Maybe a little on the inside, but they sure didn't show it. We told them we had big ideas and to trust us, and they did.

We got to work without really knowing what we were doing, googling things like, *"How do we legally start a business? How do we get a business license? How do we get a resale certificate?"* We had no one ahead of us to guide us; we just had to figure it out. And that's exactly what we did. We took a class teaching different chalk painting techniques, and I still have the board we painted that day hanging in my office. I will always cherish it.

After that, we felt like we were officially ready to launch this thing. We developed our business plan and even presented it to our husbands and parents to get their stamp of approval. Only one problem: we didn't have any real money to speak of to start a business. And that's kind of an important piece to this.

So, we typed up the best business proposal ever and presented it to my parents. A few lines worth sharing are these:

> ***Why we need you:*** *We are going to start small, so we don't need a lot of capital to begin with. But with that being said, there are startup costs, and… CONGRATULATIONS! We want you to be our investor!*
> *You are our shark. (Get it? Shark Tank!)*

You might be saying, 'But what's in it for me?'
The answer: the pure joy and satisfaction of seeing your two
wonderful, amazing daughters happy and successful in all areas of
life!
So what do you say? Are you in on this life-changing opportunity?

And guess what? They said yes. Of course they did. We needed $6,000 to get started, and my parents now say it was, *hands down*, the best investment they have ever made. I'll be forever thankful for their generosity and belief in us.

> Behind every dreamer is someone who believed in them before they believed in themselves.

I can see now that our parents and husbands did just that.

Our goals were to create custom furniture, and we also wanted to try becoming a vendor in a local store where we could sell our furniture and other decor collections. We could visualize what this would look like, and we truly couldn't wait to get started.

We named our business Wilshire Collections. Wilshire Way was a street that we grew up on, and we knew we wanted to bring it back to our roots. Our mom has a fabulous eye for design and decorating, which is 100 percent where we get that from.

Our dad was a hardworking businessman, but he also had a creative side and would take up woodworking and other projects on the side. I know 100 percent that my love for decorating and creating came from them, and for that, I'm forever grateful, because it turns out that is my passion and my calling. Who would have thought all those trips to TJ Maxx with my mom as a young girl were really just training me for my future as a professional "whisper-shopper"? (More on that later.)

I can't thank my parents enough for not only passing down those traits but also for laying the foundation of going after your dreams and working hard. They are some of the proudest parents I know, and their love for the Wilshire community and me shines through.

In March of 2013, we officially launched Wilshire Collections, two sisters with a paintbrush and a dream and a God who was much bigger than we could have imagined. Blair and I ended up applying to rent a booth at a local store. I'll never forget the feeling of finding out we got accepted.

We were over the moon. I vividly remember setting up our first vendor booth and how proud we were. Then, when the first sales came in, it felt like, *Oh my Lanta, this is actually happening!* Over time, we ended up adding a second location in a different city close by.

We were having so much fun with this new little adventure. It was fun to help people decorate their homes on a budget by offering different decor items, hand-painted pieces, and more! Not everyone has it in their budget to go out and buy a new piece of furniture (including us during those days), so it was all about taking old stuff people were getting rid of at garage sales and giving it new life on a budget.

We would do holiday markets and really started making a name for ourselves in our local community. We stayed very busy with custom-furniture clients, and word of mouth was huge for us then.

We honestly weren't too reliant on social media at that point. Looking back, I can see that even before websites and before Facebook groups, God was planting seeds for something so much bigger.

From the very start, I remember my husband, Anthony, being so supportive. He knew as well as I did how much I needed this creative outlet. Many times he went with me to garage sales looking for furniture, picked things up for me from strange houses, hauled things to the stores with me, helped set them up and stage them, and more, all with zero complaints.

Anthony is like the human version of a golden retriever, and for this, he was no different. Always happy to be there with a smile on his face and bringing me that unconditional love. Sometimes, I think I got more annoyed with the hauling and loading than he did.

Don't get me wrong, we had some moments too. There was the time I was taking a picture of a custom headboard I had painted right before the client was coming to pick it up. I had it leaned against the side of a house when a big gust of wind came, knocked it over, and cracked it.

OMG, the panic and horror set in for both of us. Luckily, she was not only very nice and understanding, but with Anthony's handy help, we were able to repair and fix it. But it did mean I had to repaint it, too. That wasn't the only oopsie moment I had along the way, and it definitely wasn't the only failure.

But all of these things make you stronger and more resilient, and without Anthony telling me to keep going, I might have run for the hills during some of those failures. It was only a headboard, but that day I learned something I'd need again and again: things break, and we repair them, and in the fixing, we get stronger too.

> Every stumble has a purpose. God can use what broke you to build you stronger.

That time, I broke a bed, but there would be other moments of brokenness to come.

This time in Wilshire was perfect for that stage of my life because my oldest son, Parker, was in elementary school, and my youngest son, Tyler, was just a little toddler. I can remember putting Tyler down for a nap, running out to the garage to paint with the baby monitor by my side, and getting as much done during nap time as I could. He quickly became my sidekick, often out there with me while I painted and worked. I would give him an old piece of wood and a paintbrush and let him help me along the way. I would take both boys to garage sales with me on the weekends, letting them buy little toys while I hunted for furniture. I truly have such fond memories of that time.

Setting up for our holiday show each year was one of my favorite things from that time period of our business. Getting to meet people as they came to shop, some who followed us and some who didn't, was always icing on the cake. There's a full-circle moment to come later in the book about our last couple of holiday shows that were held in a beautiful barn venue.

We would take several pieces of furniture up to our booth on a Thursday, and by Sunday, they were calling to say, "Bring more. You sold them all." We honestly could barely keep up at times, but somehow, by the grace of God, we made it work, and we were loving every minute of it.

Blair would paint from her garage, and I from mine. Both of us were moms with dreams of being there for our kids, but also doing something for our families and ourselves. We continued on for several years doing just that, and I like to think we got pretty good at it over the years. I'm super blessed to be so close to my sister, and this gave us an even stronger bond. We truly did work so well together.

With that being said, it was great for us for a season. In 2015, Blair's life and goals were shifting. She had already had her first son, and they were looking to grow their family even more. At that time, she decided to focus on having babies and take a step back.

It was a bittersweet time, but one I fully supported and understood, as I, too, had been in that spot before, wanting to be fully present and there for my boys when they were little. Those early years of Wilshire taught me grit, grace, and the joy of creating, but they were only the beginning of something I couldn't have seen coming. What started in November 2012 with one little jar of chalk paint became the spark that changed everything.

We had discovered a shared love for creating and had dreamed right there on the floor of our parents' house on Christmas Day about turning that into something more. Without experience or a real plan, we stepped out. We built Wilshire Collections from scratch.

Two sisters with paintbrushes and determination. Those early days were full of laughter, late nights, garage-painting marathons, and a whole lot of learning by doing. There were triumphs like getting our first booths and selling out of furniture, and there were tears, like the cracked headboard moment, spilled jars of paint, and more. But each experience made us stronger.

Those years weren't just about paint and furniture. I can see now that they were about finding purpose. They taught us resilience, creativity, and partnership.

Even more, they revealed how God can use ordinary beginnings to prepare us for something extraordinary. What felt like a small business at first was really the first step toward the community and calling that He was already writing for my life and Blair's too. Blair is now running her own amazing and successful business, BeStyled Co., helping women get dressed with ease.

She and her team offer style consults, shopping sessions, closet organizing, and more. She has her own incredible following and a community of ladies who not only look to her for fashion advice, but for the same joy that so many Wilshire ladies look for here. I love that she is now doing exactly what she's meant to do, while I am doing what I'm meant to do.

I have no doubt that was the plan back then, even when we didn't see it yet. I decided to continue on with Wilshire on my own after she left and kept plugging away just like we did when she was there. I'll always be thankful for those early days with her because, to be honest, I'm not sure I would have done it alone.

I don't think I would have been brave enough to go for it without her by my side, and to this day, she's still one of my biggest cheerleaders in life and for Wilshire. I'll never be able to thank you enough, Blair, for both the then and the now.

I have to say, being a stay-at-home mom was the biggest blessing for all those years I was able to do that, but deep down, I knew God still had something else tucked inside me, waiting to bloom.

I felt like I had the best of both worlds: getting to be with my boys, going to all their school activities and sports, having playdates with friends, and more, all while doing this side hustle in the nooks and crannies of motherhood. I hope my boys look back on the beginning of this Wilshire journey and remember a mom who loved them hard and was there for them, but one who also wasn't afraid to go after her dreams and do big things. I hope they realize they are my *why* and what kept me going so many times.

I hope that when Anthony looks back, he realizes all those hours of hauling furniture around and loading and unloading were worth it. I hope he sees that we had to go through those beginnings to get to where we are now, and I hope he realizes none of this would have been possible without his love and support. I hope when my parents look back, they're proud of those little girls they raised to be dreamers, girls they raised to step out in faith and do things even when they felt big and scary.

I hope they see how their love for our family and us has now been passed down to our own families. If I could sit down with 2013 Stacey, I'd probably say, "Oh my Lanta, girl, you won't believe this." Then we would laugh a little, and cry a little too. I'd tell her that the paint-stained hands and late nights in the garage were worth it, that the small beginnings and moments of doubt were all part of a much bigger story. I'd tell her that one jar of chalk paint would lead to a purpose she couldn't even imagine, one that would reach far beyond furniture and decor. I'd remind her that she's going to walk through some hard seasons, ones that make her question everything, but that God's hands would never leave her through any of it.

I'd tell her to keep trusting that nudge in her heart: to stay faithful in the small things and to believe that what she's building isn't just a business. It's a community, a ministry, and a living testimony of God's goodness. And then I'd probably give her a big old hug and say, "You have no idea how big this is going to be, but God does."

Before I go into what happened next with Wilshire and me, I need you to know that this isn't my story. Sure, I'm the one putting the words on the pages, but the truth is, this book is about God's faithfulness and what He's done through an online community that I never could have built on my own. I'm just the vessel He chose to use.

What started with decorating and crafting turned into something so much bigger. Women found joy, hope, healing, and friendship when they needed it most.

Like I said, I never set out to build a big business. I never set out to lead a community. Honestly, I just wanted to create, to find a little joy and a creative escape in the midst of motherhood.

But God had other plans.

> And He doesn't ask us to see the whole path, just to take that first step in faith.

God knew then what I know now: This is bigger.

CHAPTER 2
HOPE IN HARD TIMES

What happened next was full of twists and turns I didn't see coming, some good and some not so good. I went down to only being in one store, since it was just me trying to keep up, and I was still doing custom-painted pieces as well.

I also started making and selling Lazy Susan trays at that time that became a big hit very quickly. It was a struggle to keep up. I began to feel burnout since I had to physically be in my garage, painting furniture or staining trays, in order to make any kind of income. And then, something began to happen spontaneously and organically.

I slowly started to pivot and lean into my love of decorating. Keep in mind, I have zero professional training or schooling in decorating. As I mentioned before, my mom has an amazing eye for it, and I know I learned from her along the way. She definitely passed that eye on to me.

But let me tell you, my decorating did not always look the way it does now. It was something I studied by reading blogs, scouring Pinterest, and of course, through trial and error in my own home. But then something started to happen.

I would be at someone's house to give them a quote on a custom-painted piece of furniture, and they would start asking me for decorating advice. "What type of curtain should I use? What size rug do I need?" etc.

And it got me thinking: *maybe I should add this to the services I provide.* One thing you'll see throughout this book is that pretty much everything I have done in my business I've done scared and before I felt ready.

So, in 2016, I decided to launch a part of Wilshire focused on interior styling services. Talk about major impostor syndrome. Who was I? I was not an interior designer. I didn't go to school for that. Why would someone pay me to decorate their home?

But guess what? They did. I jumped in feet first and started helping people update and redecorate their homes.

Here's the thing about being an expert in your field: there are always people who know less than you do on any given subject. So, if someone didn't find joy in decorating or didn't feel like they were good at it, having me help them was a step above that.

I was always just honest with people: "Yes, I can help you, but I'm not an interior designer." And you know what? No one seemed bothered by that. It was all in my head that this was going to be an issue with people when clearly it wasn't. I've learned that feeling unqualified is often the first sign you're exactly where God wants to use you.

And we were never meant to stay inside our comfort zones. While this was way out of my comfort zone, it was also a very fun time and gave me a lot of experience with different decorating styles. It ended up being much harder than I anticipated for a variety of reasons, but the lessons it taught me and what it brought next made me realize it was a stepping stone into the next part of the plan.

Before I knew it, another shift was happening. I realized that when I shared before-and-after pictures on Facebook, some people who followed me weren't local. I started getting decorating questions in my

DMs and on posts. People wanted my help from afar, but at the time, I couldn't grasp how to do that.

- *What do you mean someone in Texas wants my advice?*
- *How can I do that?*
- *How can I help people outside of my local community?*

So, in 2017, I decided to start a blog. I've always loved to write, and I thought it would be a great way to share stories and pictures of projects I was doing, both in my own home and in those of others. Once again, I did it scared and also did it a little stupidly.

I would never recommend this to others, but I built my original WordPress blog entirely on my own, with a zero tech background. I bought an ebook on how to start a blog and followed it step by step. There were late nights, lots of tears, and plenty of mistakes made, but I was determined.

In January 2017, I launched my blog and started posting regularly, wanting to grow my following beyond my local community. It was slow growth, but every day I would post and keep trying.

I was sharing my budget-friendly decorating advice and tips, and people seemed to be enjoying it all! However, I was still painting furniture at the time. The physical toll it was taking on me and the burned-out feeling were getting worse by the day.

Around that time in 2017, my friend and biz buddy Stacey H. introduced me to the fact that there were online business coaches you could learn from, and other online business owners you could connect with. I had no idea! My eyes were opened when I found my first business coach and began networking and making those connections.

Up until that point, it had just been me, myself, and Google, learning how to do all the things. It became clear pretty quickly that this online business I was trying to grow was missing one pivotal thing: a true sense of community connection.

To build that community, it meant I needed to go Live on video. I thought, *What?* My immediate response was a powerful "*no.*"

Every time my business coach would talk about how important it was, I'd think to myself, *There's no way I'll ever do that, not in a million years.* I was feeling like a prisoner in my garage, and the physical toll of painting furniture and making Lazy Susan trays was catching up with me. I knew something had to change. I needed a major pivot in my business.

The more I learned about the importance of going Live, the more I realized that was the missing link I needed if I really wanted to pivot and make this work. People buy from people they know, like, and trust. And how were they ever going to truly get to know me if I didn't become forward-facing in my business? At that point, I rarely even posted pictures of myself, much less put myself out there in a video. I realized I was once again going to have to set my fears aside if I truly wanted to do this.

Personally, I was struggling at this time in my life. In 2017, I had a health scare that shook me to my core. I had what I originally thought was a stroke and was rushed to the ER. From there, I went to countless doctors in Nashville, every neurologist, every type of specialist, and had every kind of test run. I was a medical mystery. Yet I continued to have these episodes regularly, and no one could figure out why. When these episodes occurred, they would last about thirty seconds to a minute. One whole side of my face would draw up. My eye would close and begin to twitch, my mouth would tighten and pull upward. After it was over, I'd feel like I had been hit by a semi. My eye would continue twitching for the next twenty-four hours. These episodes truly drained me.

It started to affect my quality of life. I didn't want to go places for fear of having an episode in public. I became depressed and discouraged, to say the least. This wasn't my first rodeo with being a medical mystery. I had experienced other issues in the past that either never got resolved or took years to diagnose. I was nearly at the end of my rope with this one, almost two years in, thinking once again that no one would ever figure it out.

I had doctors tell me I was psychotic, literally their exact words, or that I was making these episodes up. They thought it was MS, then they thought it was migraines, then stress. But when I had multiple episodes on a family vacation while sitting and looking at the ocean in the Bahamas, I knew these were not brought on just by stress.

So I continued to fight for answers. I continued to find new doctors. And for anyone who has walked the road of not having answers, I always say that sometimes the not knowing is harder than finally knowing what the condition is. Once you know, you can set a plan, you can get help, you can try. Being in the limbo of not knowing only added to my depression, on top of the crippling episodes.

After two years of having these episodes multiple times a week with no answers or solutions, I finally landed with a specialist in 2019, who diagnosed me with hemifacial spasm. The reason no one else could get to the bottom of it is that it's rare, and I also didn't have a typical case. Most people start with constant twitching on one side of their face, which eventually leads to temporary paralysis.

Mine started off with aggressive episodes and paralysis, which is highly atypical. This doctor had never seen a case like mine but was confident in what it was. After reading about it and joining an online support group, I realized that, yep, there are others just like me. And while my progression wasn't typical, it was still the same condition, and many had it far worse than I did at that point.

Hemifacial spasm is caused by pressure on a main facial nerve, and at that time, I was told the only options to fix it were an invasive surgery or Botox to relax the muscle and stop the episodes. I opted for the Botox, and I'm thankful to say it worked, and that to this day, it still works. If I go without it, the episodes come back. I thank God all the time for leading me to answers and a solution. There's a very good chance that one day the Botox will stop working, but I'll cross that bridge if I come to it. For now, I'm counting my blessings.

But considering the place I was in, the thought of going on video for social media was terrifying. I couldn't bear the thought of going Live while having one of those episodes and how embarrassing it would be. I've also always struggled with my weight and body image, so I thought everyone would be throwing tomatoes at their phones as they watched me. The fears I had around being Live on Facebook were raw and real. I had no confidence in myself, in who I was, or even in what I had to teach or say at that point.

But one day in late 2017, before I was diagnosed or receiving Botox, I decided I wasn't going to let that fear control my life. If I wanted to grow this business, I simply had to put myself out there, so I did just that.

I remember being so nervous, rehearsing what I was going to say in the shower, and asking some friends and family to show up and watch the Live so I wasn't talking to anyone. And guess what? I did it. I showed up Live, sitting at my kitchen table. No one (that I know of) threw a tomato at me, and I didn't have an episode.

There weren't many people watching at all, but I did it anyway, and then I kept doing them. At first, I would just get on and talk or decorate something. Then one day in the fall of 2018, I got on and painted some Dollar Tree pumpkins. That was the start of leaning into the creative and crafty side of my business, beyond just furniture painting.

The more Live sessions I did while crafting, the more people started to actually watch and ask for more. Brooke R. from Re-Fabbed believed in me early on and asked me to go Live to craft on her page, which introduced me to even more ladies who are now part of my community. Those business friends I had made were sharing my videos, and I was doing the same for them. Together, we were all going Live and doing it scared!

When I tell you I was so nervous being on camera back then, I mean it. I wasn't showing up as my true self yet because I thought I had to be perfect and curated. That was exhausting.

I eventually realized that it's harder to show up as someone else every day than it is to let your guard down and just be you.

The moment I stopped pretending and started showing up as myself, everything changed. It was when I let that guard down and started letting my community in that everything started to shift. I was drawing in people who liked me for *me*. They didn't care what size my body was, that I was a hot mess express, and I bet they wouldn't have cared if I had an episode while Live, although that was still a great fear. They loved what I was sharing and *how* I was sharing it, so I kept showing up.

And over time, I started to laugh more, tell stories, make jokes, let my hot-mess side show, and everything in between. I was letting my guard down a little more each time I hit that "Go Live" button.

But even as I started becoming more *me*, one huge thing was still happening in the background: those episodes and my ongoing health struggles. And I continued to face the true, raw fear of having one while I was Live. But you know what? God protected me from one of my greatest fears, and I never did have an episode on video. There were so many times I would literally hit the end button and have one right after, but He protected me from that happening publicly. No one who followed me even knew what I was going through at the time.

I was finding hope in hard times, and my community was supporting me in ways I never knew they could. This became so special to me because this little community I was slowly growing was healing me. They were helping me come out of my depression and helping me find a purpose again, and they didn't even have a clue how much they were helping me through this hard time in my life with health struggles. Because again, *no one* except family and close friends knew about this battle I was fighting back then.

I now know that behind the scenes, the same thing was happening for many other ladies from my community. They were being helped and lifted up during hard times, too, like Missy S., whose story I told in the beginning. There were others like Missy and me: some whose stories they shared with me along the way and some whom I just heard for the first time while collecting stories for this book.

I love how God is always working in the background, even when we may not know it at the time. We may not ever know, and that's okay. There are so many people whose lives are being touched by you daily who may never speak it back to you.

There are lives we are impacting without knowing we are doing so, and that is truly so special. I've encountered so many touching stories like this directly myself, and I would like to share a few with you.

———

LORI L.'S STORY

I've always loved to decorate and craft, and when doing so, I'm in one of my happy places. In 2021, I was diagnosed with breast cancer. When you hear the C word, your whole life is turned upside down.

I had surgery, and my radiation started in November. I remember sitting there one day, just lost in the fact that my life would never be the same. My kids, I thought. They still need a mom.

Would I live to see my newborn grandbaby grow up? Would my new husband continue to love me? He didn't sign up to take care of me and withstand all the devastating side effects treatment can cause.

All the same things were just swirling in my head. I was scrolling Face-book, and a video of something from Wilshire Collections was in my feed. I don't remember exactly what, but it involved Christmas, and Stacey was talking and explaining about Christmas being her favorite.

I can't even tell you what she said. I just remember thinking I was meant to see this. I felt at peace.

I felt like I liked her, and she was relatable, and I needed more of this in my life. So I binge-stalked the Wilshire page. It wasn't even about the craft or video. It was something about her. I remember telling my husband, "I think if Stacey and I lived closer to each other, we would really be friends."

Every day for a month, I had radiation except on weekends and Thanksgiving Day. Radiation made me really tired, so I found that every day afterward, I would lie down and scroll the Wilshire page for the daily post. I still have to take meds for the cancer and will for some years to come, but that's okay. I've now been cancer-free for four years.

I took Stacey's Decorating 101 class, and then joined the Decorating and Creating Community, and now she is part of my daily life. I love to watch her go Live, not only for the crafts and the home tours and decorating, but everyone is sweet and supportive.

She truly makes you feel like you matter and are family. I love the fact that she allows prayer posts, and I also love the positive-only atmosphere. We need more of that in the world.

I'm doing well now, but I'm telling you, thanks to the Wilshire family, I've made it through some hard times, and don't tell anyone, but she may have brought some of the Christmas magic back for me that day, too.

———

Wow, what a powerful story!

There's another Lori who also has a story that speaks volumes!

———

LORI S.'S STORY

I've always loved crafting. For as long as I can remember, from my teens until now, I would often crochet, paint ceramics, make floral arrangements, etc. In 2016, my whole world was totally rocked and changed forever.

What should have been a totally normal day with my husband turned out anything but. I received a call at work in the afternoon that the love of my life had collapsed at work and was being rushed to the hospital.

Within three hours after arriving, I said goodbye to my best friend of thirty-four years. He had suffered a catastrophic aortic aneurysm.

He was only 58. I was shocked, absolutely heartbroken, and devastated. That one day sent me into a spiral of not really having a desire to do anything. Depression was setting in, and it was deep.

I could put on a pretty brave front and smile when I had to, but inside, the loss was paralyzing. There were days I would stay in bed for hours on end and cry until I couldn't cry anymore.

Over time, I would find myself hopping on Facebook occasionally to see what was going on. I stumbled upon the Wilshire Collections. Stacey's positivity and upbeat nature were evident, not to mention the off-the-charts ideas on decorating.

I began to follow, and for a time, I found it healing and encouraging just to have that sound of someone talking to me about something. To me, it was almost as though someone was in the house with me, keeping me company. Little by little, I started to come out of that deep place of sadness that had overtaken my life and began to look forward to something again.

My passion and love for crafting and decorating were being ignited once again through Stacey. I loved listening to the funny stories on there that made me laugh, and awkward life moments, or the whisper-shopping that showed realism, only made me love the site even more. In a world where there is a lot of phony baloney, I could tell that was not the case here.

Stacey is as real as they come, caring, open, and it's obvious she loves what she does, her family, and her faith. I saw so much talent on her Facebook page, I found myself finally looking forward to something again. I couldn't wait for another video to drop.

Between this site and my church connection, I felt myself, after a long time, finally coming out of a pit. I joined her Decorating and Creating Community, where a sense of community is evident. Stacey has no idea the effect she has had on my life and how watching her has brought back some of the things I love into my home.

Thank you, Stacey, for the love and hope you share every time you are on, even when you yourself are struggling with life events. I'm not sure you have an idea of what you mean to some of us watching. It's inspirational, and I can't imagine not being a part of this community and, of course, seeing what's coming next.

PAMELA H.'S STORY

I'm a 53-year-old woman who has been permanently disabled for over twenty years. I've previously worked four jobs to raise my two boys as a single mom.

In three of these jobs, I was able to work from home as I did medical transcription, so I was able to work around their schedules. When I found out I could no longer work, I had a deep depression and needed to find my way out. I needed to figure out something I could do for myself by myself so that I didn't need to rely on anyone for help.

I always enjoyed crafting, but due to my extreme workload and caring for two young boys, I can honestly say I had to set all of that on the back burner. My boys grew up, which left me with more availability. I began watching some crafting videos again.

There were a couple that stuck with me right from the start. I really liked their style, their down-to-earth atmosphere, true life stories, honesty, sincerity, and all-around well-being and personality. Stacey, you've been one of those crafters that I've stuck with from the very beginning of my journey.

You are family-oriented and down-to-earth. I love your story time as much as I love your crafts. You really know how to brighten up someone's day when they're down.

It's really been amazing to be a follower of your page and a PC girl as long as I have. You've helped me in so many ways out of a dark hole that I was in and to get myself back into something I know I can do and enjoy. It may take me longer than others to complete certain projects, but I'm okay with that, as I know I have to do only what my body can handle, take a break, and come back to it later rather than get frustrated.

Watching and listening to you has taught me so much over the past several years, and for that, I'm truly grateful. You're a true inspiration.

───────

I have no doubt that there are hundreds of other stories to be told just like these ladies', and there will be more along the way as well. When I think back to "2017 me," the girl with zero confidence, the girl who was struggling with her own health and was scared and depressed, the girl who pushed past her fears because her dreams were bigger, well, I'm proud of her. She could have stopped it all right then, thrown in the towel, and been done. But she didn't.

She kept going. At that moment, she didn't know her path or what the future would hold, but God did. Thank goodness she leaned in and listened, because she wouldn't be writing this book today if she hadn't.

I was so lucky to have so many supportive family members, friends, and business friends by my side to cheer me on and help me along the way during that time. I know without a shadow of a doubt that I wouldn't be where I am today if I hadn't pushed past that fear and had God by my side. Can you imagine how different my life would be if I had never been brave enough to hit that "Go Live" button? That button: it changed everything.

Because when I started opening up, going Live, and growing into the authentic version of myself, that's when it all began to click. That's when I really started growing a community. I kept showing up at my kitchen table week after week. I started letting them into my life and my personality.

I started to gain a little confidence, though still not a ton back then, and I started to become obsessed with this little community I was building. Little did I know then what an impact it was starting to have and would continue to have. You could have never told me that "2026 me" would now hop on a Live without thinking twice, show up as my true, authentic, hot-mess self, and even embarrass myself from time to time. (Oh, do I have some stories to share!)

When I started going Live, I told myself, *If it's horrible and people throw tomatoes at me, I don't have to keep doing them. But I won't know until I try.* And trying changed it all. What I wasn't expecting during that time was how much of an outlet it would become for me. Because during that hour or so, I wasn't "depressed Stacey" who had these crazy facial episodes. I was just "Stacey," laughing, smiling, and sharing what I love. I was thinking about this community I was building, how I could serve them, and whatever project we were working on. Slowly, I was healing, all because I did it scared. I'll forever be proud that I took that leap of faith.

If you find yourself in a similar situation, where you know there's something you want to do that would be good for you, but you're scared to do it, you just have to *do it scared.* That's a theme you'll see over and over again in this book. If you sit around and wait for the perfect time... well, often there never is a perfect time.

You can't wait until you have the perfect words. Or wait until you're not fighting health problems. Or wait until you lose the weight, or whatever it is.

> You just have to take the leap, trust, and figure the rest out as you go.

I went from rehearsing what I was going to say in the shower and shaking like a leaf each time I hit that "Go Live" button to slowly becoming more and more myself with each Live I did. That vulnerability started to change my business, and it turns out God knew that hitting the "Go Live" button was going to change my life. That *this* was going to be bigger all along.

CHAPTER 3
THE IMPACT OF INFLUENCE

I 'm going to say this even though I do not like the word: *influencer.* Ugh.

Why is there such a stigma around that word? It makes me cringe a bit. Why?

Because sometimes, when you hear "influencer," you think of someone who shares products, trying to make a dime. But that's honestly far from the truth for most influencers.

As I began to grow my community, the shift from the girl in her garage painting furniture to the girl online "influencing" started to happen.

I consider myself way more than an influencer, but I do know I have influence.

Do I influence people to go shop and buy cute things I share? Yep, I sure do. Do I influence them to see how much they *need* printables, pillows, or other cute items that I sell? Yep, definitely. But I've also influenced them to become part of this community, to open up in ways they maybe haven't in a long time, and to lean into their creativity and their passions. I've influenced them to find joy in their lives and to be proud of their homes.

Influencers can be very misunderstood. But when you look at the heart of the community behind influencers like me, you'll see that it's so much more than you might think. Is that true for every influencer out there? I'm sure it's not. But I can tell you that I've been lucky enough to meet several others in a similar online space, and the heart behind what we do, and why we do it, is all the same.

In my opinion, the best kind of platform is one that lifts others up and makes them feel welcomed. I hope that I can debunk the stigma around influencers a bit as you continue to read and see that there's truly so much more to this type of job. It's a job far from normal by traditional standards, but one I truly believe will help shape the future.

> True influence isn't measured by followers or sales. It's measured by lives touched and hearts encouraged. Influence becomes *impact* when it points people back to hope, joy, and community.

But here's the thing: not everyone will get it. People who do what I do will be talked about, judged, and sometimes even made fun of.

I didn't follow a safe path. I opened doors that no one could see or understand except me. But I did it, not because it was easy, not because anyone guaranteed me success, but because I had a vision, a dream, and the guts to go after it.

Remember, you're seeing a *highlight reel* from the people you follow on social media: the best of the best five to ten minutes of their entire day, the curated photos, and perfectly styled spaces. What people don't see are the impostor syndrome battles, the late nights, the tears, the tech issues, the failures, and the messy, real-life moments.

You only see what they put out, and you often see influencers in a perfect light, which is far from the truth for most. I will say I've had the best support from family and friends over the years. I'm surrounded by people who have nothing but love and encouragement for me. But I'd be lying if I said I haven't also been hurt and lost friendships along the way.

Some people will never get it. They'll never understand why you want more for your life. They'll never understand why you'd put yourself out there in such a public way. Some people get jealous. Some even stab you in the back. It's an unfortunate part of life, and it's been one of the hardest and most painful parts of running this business.

I've struggled over the years to own what I do when talking to people outside this space. I would downplay it when acquaintances would say, "How's your little crafting thing going? Are you having fun doing your little crafts every day?"

I wish all I did was craft all day, but I would simply reply, "Yeah, it's going good, just staying busy," and then quickly change the subject. Why do we, as women (and maybe some men too), not feel confident and comfortable enough to own it? To say, "Yes, you know what? It's going amazingly, and I get to spread joy every day to ladies everywhere and help them with their homes." Instead, we play it small.

But here's the thing: I wasn't doing this business to play it small, and I had to decide that I wasn't going to downplay what I was doing for others anymore. I was going to let them watch, let them judge, and let them copy when they wanted a piece of what I was doing. Let them abandon me when they couldn't handle or couldn't understand my growth or success.

That was their problem, not mine, but it's taken me years to understand that, and it's still hard at times. But I'm here to tell you right now: I'm done playing it small. I'm done hiding what we've built together here at Wilshire.

I'm ready to shout it from the rooftops that because of God, we have something amazing going on here, and I will forever continue to sing His praises because of it. So yes, there's *impact* in the influence. God gave me this platform not so that I could be seen, but so that *others* could feel seen.

I've seen it firsthand, time and time again, and I hope you see it too throughout this book. The more I plugged along, showed up as myself, and served my community, the more the community started to grow, mostly on Facebook.

In 2018, I decided I wanted to start an online membership: my decorating community. This would be a VIP group where I would go Live with exclusive crafting and decorating tutorials. We would become a tight-knit group, and I would give them all kinds of extra perks. Oh my Lanta, I thought I was onto something, but then came the doubters again.

- "Why would someone pay you to learn things they can learn on Pinterest?"
- "How will this be sustainable year after year?"
- "What will you talk about and teach?"

I could have let that doubt stop me. Even though I didn't fully understand the impact of what I was building just yet, I knew I had to try. I'm so glad I did, because here I am, seven years later, and the Decorating and Creating Community is still going strong and thriving. The impact of influence has been proven to me time and time again through this group, as I've helped thousands and thousands of ladies over the years.

The truth is, though, that the time period when I started the DC wasn't the most fruitful season of my life. This hobby-turned-business was costing a lot of money to run but not always bringing the most back into the bank. It was slow growth, and I can remember feeling like I was on the cusp of a breakthrough. I told Anthony in 2019 that I wanted to give it one more year, and if I couldn't make it work, I would go get a job at Kirkland's.

In true Anthony fashion, he told me he had no doubt I could do it and that I could take as long as I needed. I wanted it to work. I knew I had it in me, but I also knew I couldn't work this hard and not turn it into a thriving and profitable business. That motivated me even more. I knew that where God guides, He provides, and I had to keep trusting in that. So I kept plugging along. At first, there were twenty people in the DC, but I loved them like they were two hundred.

And as I continued to plug away and talk about it, the community, which was my first subscription group, started to grow. It didn't take long at all for me to realize that it was a special little spot on the internet. They were becoming like family to me. It was becoming a safe space for all of us. You'll hear me refer to them as my "DC fam" or the "DC girls."

Each month, I do exclusive decorating and crafting tutorials there, but it's so much more than that. They are treated like true VIPs, with early access to pre-orders, discount perks, and so much more. But really, it's about the community. It's about how we can be ourselves in that Facebook group and connect with others who enjoy the same things we do. It's about being seen, heard, and loved, and it's beyond special. Over the years, we've added things like our virtual craft nights over Zoom. I joke that this took our relationship to the next level, because now we get to put faces with names and get to know each other on a more personal level.

The laughs we've had on those Zoom nights are the best. And the way we come from all walks of life, all parts of the country, even the world, and still find common ground, still form bonds, and still build friendships… that's worth its weight in gold.

One of the most powerful things we do in there is our monthly prayer thread. And because this is held in a private Facebook group, you can post in there without fear that a random friend from high school you don't talk to anymore will see your comment. When I realized how many ladies in the DC were also women of faith who turned to the group for prayer requests, we started a monthly prayer thread. It's simple: they get to come to the group and lay out their prayer requests, and we get to pray for them. How amazing to have such a safe space where you can do that and know you'll have hundreds of women praying for you. Yep, this is bigger.

I truly think this group is something you can't fully explain or do justice to until people join and see for themselves just how special it is. I don't think I'll ever be able to fully express just how much they mean to me. They've helped me on my darkest days, cheered me on, supported me on my best days, and everything in between. When I'm down, I want to talk to my DC fam. When I have good news, you bet I'm eager to tell them. They've given me advice, unwavering support, and loyalty that truly can't be put into words.

There are so many amazing women who've been part of the DC fam over the years, and it's been an honor to watch them grow and gain confidence in their decorating and DIY skills. Missy S., whose story I told earlier, was one of the early members of the DC. I knew that if I could help her, there had to be others out there I could help in the same way. I knew this had become my mission, my passion, my calling: to help others like Missy find joy in their lives and homes through decorating and DIY.

Little did I truly know that I would hear *countless* stories like that in the years to come. One of my favorite stories from the DC is that of Marlene and Gwen. Cue the song "It's a Small World After All."

Marlene and Gwen lived in the same town but didn't know each other. Both were in the Decorating and Creating Community and happened to be shopping at Hobby Lobby on the same day. Marlene was in the craft aisle, watching one of my Facebook Lives on her phone to refresh her memory on which supplies she needed, when Gwen said, "Are you watching Stacey? I follow her too!"

They began chatting and realized they were both in the DC, and lived in the same town, not far from each other at all! Not only that, but they now get together for lunch, shopping, etc., and are great friends. My favorite is when they send me a selfie from their adventures.

My prayer is that others can find these kinds of connections in the most unexpected places, like Hobby Lobby. I always joke that the ladies in my community should wear a sign that says, *"I follow Stacey with Wilshire Collections"* anytime they shop, because you just never know who else in that store might do the same. Your next bestie could be waiting for you.

You never know what God is going to put in your path or how He's going to turn what you think is just something fun into something *so much bigger.* Christy's story is a great example of that.

———

CHRISTY S.'S STORY

I've always said God works in mysterious ways, and we never know what he's going to put in front of us. When I started checking out Wilshire Collections and watching Stacey's life, it just struck me. I continued to move forward and join the DC community, and what I thought was just going to be someplace for decorating ideas.

Boy, was I wrong in a good way. What I have found in the DC is a wonderful supporting community. The DC is a sisterhood that words really cannot express.

It's a feeling of emotional support when needed, virtual hugs, and an outpouring of love. Who would have thought you would find something like that from women you have never seen or met except online? It's a place where you feel safe expressing faith and concern when someone is going through a rough time, when someone struggles, or has tears.

The immediate love and support shine through and are truly heartfelt. It does not matter where you live, what you do, or how old you are; you feel like one big family, again, going back to sisterhood.

I can be having a difficult day, and then a Live pops up and puts a smile on my face and love in my heart. For that, "thanks" does not even cover it. The inspiration I get from Stacey and others is just wonderful.

My house has never looked so put together, and even my husband noticed it. The stories that the ladies tell of meeting up by accident and making lifelong friends in one way or another, I call them "Godwinks."

———

I love a Godwink, and I also love to spread surprise blessings to the DC girls when I can. I do so many behind-the-scenes things for members, many of which will never be shared or told, but I do love this story from Malissa M. that I wanted to share.

———

MALISSA M.'S STORY

I had been in DC for years and even attended Stacey's first live event in 2019 with my daughter, and then I was diagnosed with cancer in 2021. I didn't know what my future would look like. I had to quit my job due to chemo and radiation, so I canceled all my subscriptions except my DC subscription.

I needed it. I needed the encouragement and prayers from Stacey and my other DC fam. I needed the distraction from what I was going through.

One day over the holidays while going through treatments, my family brought the mail in, and there was a package for me. It was from none other than Stacey with a handwritten card and a few gifts to bring me joy. She will never know what that meant to me during that time.

———

This was a small gesture that made a great impact on her life at that time. And, you know, it's just those little things and those small gestures that make an impact bigger than you realize sometimes.

It's such a good reminder to stop and do the little things. Drop a gift off on someone's porch when you know they're having a hard time, or pick up the phone and tell someone how much they mean to you. It could just mean the world to them. It could just make an impact.

I'm sure when Malissa joined the DC, she didn't expect to not only be diagnosed with cancer, but for the DC to become such a bright spot in her life. Malissa went on to attend two more of my live events with her daughters and is still a very special part of the DC and my life to this day.

Everyone finds the DC at different points in their lives, and sometimes it comes along when people need it most. I truly hope God brings the right people to it at the right time, just like He did for Margaret C.

———

MARGARET C.'S STORY

I lost my husband only twenty-three days after his diagnosis of stage 4 liver and lung cancer. I was absolutely lost and trying to learn how to live a life alone and without my soulmate. I was scrolling Facebook one day and ran across Stacey talking about her DC Girls and how meaningful this group was for others. I was looking for something different, and it felt like Stacey was inviting me to join a fun group that could make my life brighter.

I am very close to God, and I felt Him leading me to join. It lifted my spirits, and I looked forward to the positivity and to getting to know this young lady named Stacey. I truly feel the love and concern that Stacey and her DC group show, and I love that it is all Christian-based. She lifted me out of a dark place, took my mind off my loss, and encouraged me to look toward a brighter future.

I will always be grateful for the perfect timing of finding her and for being included in her sweet community. Thank you, Stacey, for your smile, sweet disposition, and the love you have for your DC Girls.

———

These are just a few of the stories that opened my eyes to the impact of influence, to the importance of community, and to the kind of moments that always remind me I'm right where I need to be.

Here's the thing:

> When you start walking in your purpose and living out your calling, things start to happen and align.

God gave me this platform to build a community, but I'm just the vessel. And there have been so many moments over the years where I haven't felt equipped or qualified. I still feel that way at times, but I truly know I'm walking in my purpose. And if I keep God at the center of all I do, in every shift and pivot that comes along, then I'm right where He wants me.

When I recently asked some of the DC girls to share what the group meant to them, the overwhelming theme was: it's so much more than crafting and decorating. Over and over, they described it as a family, a place where women from all over, most of whom have never met in person, feel deeply connected, supported, and loved. They talk about how this group has carried them through some of the hardest seasons of their lives, grief, loneliness, health battles, and heartbreak, and how it's also been there to celebrate their joys, milestones, and everyday victories.

For many, it's been a light in the darkness, a source of hope, laughter, and purpose when life felt heavy. They've enjoyed the behind-the-scenes glimpses of me sharing my home, my humor, my heart, my family, and my faith with them. They described the DC as a place where kindness always wins, where there's no judgment, just encouragement, prayers, and genuine friendship. They call it a sisterhood, a safe space, and a blessing. And while they love the decorating ideas, the printables, and all the fun projects, what they treasure most is the heart behind it all, the faith, the fellowship, and the sense that God Himself had a hand in bringing them together.

The Decorating and Creating Community isn't just about crafts or decorating. It's about belonging. It's where strangers become sisters, where laughter meets prayer, and where kindness fills every corner. Through creativity and connection, we've found hope, healing, and friendship. In my heart, I truly feel like people come for the decorating and crafting, but they stay for the community, which is like a sisterhood. And when I tell you later what kind of impact this community has made, you'll realize this even more.

So to the influencer haters out there, the ones who think this is a silly little job or something superficial at best, welcome to the life of the DC. Welcome to the Wilshire community as a whole. I hope your eyes are open to what truly can happen in the online space, because yes, this isn't your typical nine-to-five job, but it's just as important nonetheless.

My community as a whole, both on the main page, in the DC, and in my other subscriptions, means the world to me. Building an online community isn't about algorithms, likes, or follower counts. It's about connection. It's about creating a space where people feel seen, safe, and supported.

In a world that often feels disconnected, an online community can become a lifeline. It can reach women who may be sitting in loneliness, grief, or uncertainty, and remind them they're not alone. It's proof that God can use the internet, something as basic as Wi-Fi and a Facebook group, to do something extraordinary.

When people feel seen and valued, they show up not just for the content, but for each other. That's when a page becomes a community, a business becomes a calling, and a following becomes a family.

The online aspect of the DC is just part of what makes this community special. And I can't wait to tell you about how we've been able to come together to make an even bigger impact in the world: how some of us have met in person and formed lifelong friendships.

So while I don't love the word "influencer," I do love *being* one. I love that I get to facilitate and lead a safe place where I can love on a community of women from all across the country and make them feel special, because they are.

I love that I influence them to take time for themselves, to do what brings joy into their lives and into their homes.

I'm not here just to push my products or promote products for other brands. That's a small piece of the puzzle in a much bigger picture.

I'm here to make an impact. It's what I've been doing, and it's what I will continue to do, and I will do it with pride. I will no longer back down from shouting from the rooftops about what an impact influence can have.

So the next time someone asks me how my "little crafting business" is going, or talks about me behind my back... maybe I'll hand them a copy of this book.

Because I pray that everyone can make connections in their lives like the DC girls have made inside that Facebook group. I pray you find your people. Your joy. Your outlet.

From the very beginning, God created us for relationship with Him and with others.

Community, even online, is one of the ways we can live that out, and I'm so, so proud of the community we've built here. No matter how you're involved in this community, I have no doubt that God will continue to make it a place that women turn to for connection, for an outlet, for sisterhood. I have no doubt that He will continue to show everyone who becomes part of the DC fam or the Wilshire community in general that *this is bigger.*

That's why this community has been so important in my life: because they're people who get it. And when you're around people who get it, I have no problem shouting from the rooftops what I'm doing. But when you're around people who just don't understand your purpose, your why, or why you're doing this, it's like your natural reaction is to just say, "Yeah, I mean, it's good," and move on.

But over time, I've realized, *no, I'm not going to let them think that way.* And yes, I've made some people feel awkward. I really have. I've had people say things like, "How's your little crafting business?" And I've had to look at them and say, "Actually, it's a lot more than that. And it's going great." And the look on their face is like, *Oh my gosh, I wasn't expecting that.*

And listen, I'm very much a people pleaser. I don't like confrontation. So that's not in my comfort zone, but I'm trying more and more because I know what we've built here. And I know what God is doing in this community. He wouldn't want me to downplay this or keep it small.

It's still something I struggle with. And it's especially hard when it's someone you thought would be supportive. You think, *I thought they got it...* and then you realize they don't. That hurts. But it's a work in progress, for sure.

Surrounding yourself with people who *do* get it is so important. Some of my online business friends are truly my best friends in life, because what we do is weird and different, but we get each other. Trust me, I have friends in my everyday life who are so supportive, but there have been some along the way who just simply have not gotten it, and I had to come to terms with the fact that they never would. That's why having people in your same space, whether it's crafting, decorating, or just the online space in general, is so important.

Find like-minded people, because those are the people you can go to without fear of judgment. They'll support you. And they'll understand what it's like when the negativity comes, because unfortunately, that's part of putting yourself out there. I've had some truly hurtful and hateful things sent to me through Messenger, in the comments, you name it. If I call one of my business friends and say, "Listen to this message I just got from a follower..." they 100 percent understand. They'll say, "Girl, let it go," and offer the exact advice I need.

> Surround yourself with people who get you, people who support you, and love you unconditionally. Because they're the ones who will cheer you on during your best moments, and they'll lift you up when you're in your hardest seasons.

So, what about people who don't understand what you're doing or don't get your passion and calling? They're not the ones you'll turn to when things get hard, or even when you want to celebrate a win.

You need those *true* people. I couldn't even imagine doing all that I do to this day without those friendships that are also impacting so many lives around them. We aren't a "bunch of influencers" with no purpose behind what we do. Together, we are all making an impact, sharing our gifts with the world, all while knowing this influence we have… well… it's so much bigger than just us!

CHAPTER 4
CREATING CONNECTION THROUGH COMMUNITY

Beyond the impact of influence, so many women are also craving connection. When they find a space that welcomes them with open arms and provides laughter, prayer, and creativity, it fills a void they didn't even realize was there.

Hopefully, the previous chapter has shown you how real this connection can be. But yes, this connection is primarily online. I often laugh and tell my community it feels like a one-way street: while I am Live, I can only see myself on my phone and only their comments, not their faces as they watch. I got to know so many names of my loyal regulars who would always show up Live, but I had no idea what they looked like or really anything about them.

As crazy as it may sound, God was helping me build a family through Facebook. We were creating connections through the community, and it was amazing. Back in 2013, I could have never seen what was coming next.

Back then, I used to teach furniture painting classes locally. I can remember how much I loved those and how they filled my cup, getting to meet ladies who had similar passions and interests as I did. These were small classes with usually fewer than ten ladies at a time.

If God had told me back then that one day I would be hosting events where ladies traveled from all across the country to attend, well… I probably would have run for the hills in fear at the thought of that. But God said, "Let's do this." And in the fall of 2019, I was able to host my first in-person live crafting event.

I had seen other creators in my space host these types of events, and I'd even been a guest crafter at a couple of them. I'll never forget going to an event by Brooke from Re-Fabbed and being one of her guest crafters. It was so special.

And for the first time, I was getting to meet people from my own community, since we have some overlap in our followers. I will never forget that surreal feeling of taking pictures with people and hearing their stories. I remember leaving there and thinking, *One day, I want to have an event just like this*, even though it felt so scary and hard.

I remember Brooke encouraging me to do just that, to plan an event to bring my community together. So I did.

At that time, I had no one on my team. It was me, myself, and I running it all. So in 2019, I recruited family and friends, even a local DC girl, to help me plan and execute the event. I had no idea what I was getting myself into, but I also had no idea the reward it would bring.

This was the most eye-opening weekend because, for the first time, I was getting to host some of the ladies from the DC and from my broader online community. I was excited, but I truly didn't know what to expect. Fifty ladies from all across the country traveled to Nashville, Tennessee, to spend a couple of days crafting with me.

We had just finished setting up the room, and Anthony and I had gone up to the hotel room to freshen up and get ready before the doors opened. My sister called and told me I needed to come down because people were already lined up, waiting for the doors to open. I couldn't believe it.

We came down the elevator, and as the doors opened, I saw a sea of ladies standing and sitting there.

The ones who were sitting stood up, and they all began to clap. I remember looking around over my shoulder, thinking, *Who's here? Who are they clapping for?*

And that's when Anthony looked at me and said, "They're clapping for you."

What? Those claps were for little ol' me?

The tears came, and I couldn't believe it. At that moment, it all became so real. These ladies, whose names I had come to know over a computer screen, now had faces. I got to hug their necks, hear their stories, and spend two amazing days with them. To say I was humbled to my core is a true understatement. I knew that everything God had me doing, showing up when I was scared, had led me to that moment. I knew then I was right where I needed to be. That event changed me for the better, and I knew it wouldn't be my last.

The year 2019 was also when I realized that me, myself, and Google were not going to cut it anymore. I had Blair in the beginning, and then after that, I did it mostly alone. I had friends I would pay to help me pack up decor boxes, use their garage as a shipping hub, help me stain Lazy Susans, and prep for events, but I didn't have a true team to speak of. I did it mostly alone for far too long, but I did it… and lived to tell about it. I knew I had to get help if I truly wanted to grow the way I believed I was meant to.

At that point, I started growing my team slowly but surely, and of course, quickly wished I had done it sooner. I brought on Caity right after that 2019 event, and I originally told her I needed maybe three to five hours of help a week, but she quickly exceeded that as I realized just how much help I truly needed.

> If there's one thing I've learned from that aspect of my business, it's that we go further and faster together.

I shouldn't have to be the creative mind, *plus* the tech girl, *plus* the customer service rep, and so much more. So I found amazing people over time who had qualities and strengths that I didn't have.

I built the dream team, and to this day, I couldn't do any of this without them. This story is as much theirs as it is mine, and there will be more on that to come. I knew after that 2019 event that it wouldn't be my last.

The COVID-19 pandemic kept me from hosting an event for the following two years, but in 2022, I was finally able to host a small event: the DC Getaway. This was a VIP event with twenty ladies from my DC group. Each one showed up not knowing a single person.

We spent an amazing day together, and instant bonds and connections were formed. This day was so different from my 2019 event, but in the best way. I never could have dreamed of the friendships that would form from that gathering.

To this day, those ladies are still in a Facebook Messenger chat together, where they keep up with each other. They've even coordinated staying at the same hotel or booking Airbnbs together for my future events. Some of them chat daily and have become true besties. And guess what? I got to form some really close friendships with many of them, too. Some of them have helped me in more ways than I could ever express, and I know they know exactly who they are. They were a light in my life that I didn't even know I needed at that time. I have no doubt that God put the people in that room who needed to be there that day.

Here's the thing I've learned about creating new friendships in adulthood: they're hard to find and sometimes even harder to keep. So many friendships are built during a season or time period in your life and are somewhat circumstantial.

But these friendships are lasting because they're built on a common bond and shared interests. So for anyone who says online friendships aren't real, I challenge them to come to one of these events and see for themselves.

JANICE H.'S STORY

I was a silent watcher at first. I joined the Printable Club when it first started. Shortly after, I joined the DC. Then, as soon as the Pillow Cover Club started, I jumped right in. I trusted Stacey from the very beginning. She was so down-to-earth and funny. She was exactly what I needed and didn't even know it, especially when 2020 hit.

When she talked about the DC Getaway, I was all in, scared and excited, but all in. And I thank God all the time that I went. I did not know a single person when I walked into that beautiful venue.

It was so far out of my comfort zone, it wasn't even funny. But that's where it all started. Meeting Stacey in person was like meeting a lost relative.

A warmer welcome from a more genuine person couldn't have happened. We had fun crafting, and I met and talked to everyone there, which was very much out of my comfort zone. Having Anthony and their boys there was proof positive of how family and faith-based this community is.

The bus ride to Kirkland's and the Mercantile, then to the townhouse, was next level in friendship-making for me. I sat with a girl I swore was so much younger than me, and I wondered if we would have anything in common. As it turned out, we had more in common than I thought, and we are now more like sisters, as I don't have any.

We laugh so hard and still do when we talk about that trip. I will never forget those memories. I had never done anything like this in my life.

I've met and become so close to a few of the ladies, "sister friends" I call them, and we message daily. More memories were made at the next two events to follow Wilshire Live. Those friendships grew deeper, all because of Stacey.

Meeting her family again was such a treat, along with her team. I know when I talk to friends and family about these events, they don't quite get it, but they see how much I enjoy crafting, love the friends I've made, and continue to make new ones. Wilshire, Stacey, and the Collins family have become more important to me than I could have ever imagined a crafting video could be.

God puts people in your life for a reason, that's for sure. A reason I never knew I needed.

───────

Flash forward to 2023, when I hosted my biggest event yet with 100 ladies traveling from over 25 states to attend.

Not only did this require help from my team, but I also hired an event planner for this one. Kellie, who works for me and is the only team member who lives locally, packed every single craft kit and talked through every detail of the event with me. It takes a true village to put on events of this size, and I'm so thankful for mine.

I have so many amazing memories from that event, from the VIP dinner and shopping night (where Kirkland's closed the store just for us so we could shop till we dropped), to the two incredible days of crafting and getting to know each other even better. I know I mentioned my village and support, so I have to take a moment to talk about my family, who always shows up for everything I do. Having Anthony and the boys there, not only to help but to meet the ladies and witness the goodness of God, was truly so special.

My parents and sister are always there cheering me on, and Anthony's family came to be part of it too. One of my favorite videos from this event is of my parents standing in the back of the room with their arms around each other as I stood on stage and closed out the event, speaking to a room full of ladies standing, clapping, crying, and making heart shapes with their hands. To see it from my parents' perspective was to witness their pride and love through a completely different lens.

The ladies at these events were forming real friendships, and they were even making sure some of the husbands who tagged along had something to do while we crafted.

TERESA'S S.'S STORY

I discovered Wilshire Collections after my mom had a stroke in 2020.

I was scrolling on Facebook, and it popped up, so I checked it out. It was like it was meant to be. Because of the stroke, COVID, and trying to take care of everything else, I was getting a little depressed.

I started watching Stacey's videos and realized that I could start crafting while being with Mom and Dad, so that's what I did. I love Stacey's page. I love the printables.

Watching her videos and Lives helps me so much. I'm so thankful for finding her page. When she mentioned the 2023 live event in Franklin, I told my husband, Bo, he could get me that for Christmas, and he did because he supports me in my crafting.

He decided to go with me, but asked if I could check the FB page to see if any husbands would like to play golf while we were doing our stuff. We got a few of the ladies who said their husbands would like to play, and that's how the Wilshire Golfers came about. From that golf outing, that's how we met Marco and Katrina B., Scott and Tammy C., and Kelly and Debbie W. We all became lifelong friends.

We've even gotten together with Marco and Katrina since then, and now we go on trips with them. At the 2025 live event, there were even more golfers, and I've also met more amazing women. I'm excited to see what Wilshire Live 2026 brings.

I love being part of this community, Stacey. You and your team are special people. You're all the same in person as you are on Facebook.

You have such a heart and care for us all so much. You have a wonderful family that I'm glad I got to meet. I love going on your journeys with you.

I love the funny and hilarious stories, and I love that I found Wilshire Collections back in 2020. Thank you for helping me through some hard times.

_____

While the golfers were away, we spent a couple of days making some adorable projects, but we always sprinkle in other impactful and fun things as well. We did an activity that was so impactful, one where we wrote "You Are Letters." Each lady wrote a letter to someone else in the room, starting with "You."

They were encouraged to write words that would lift someone up, things like *"You are amazing," "You are worthy," "You are loved,"* etc. They thought they would be passing them down to someone else, but instead, we told them to open the letters and read them to themselves. That letter they wrote for someone else was actually for *them*. It was the message they needed to hear. There weren't many dry eyes in the room at that point.

One of my favorite memories from that event happened at the very end, when I was saying my goodbyes. I got emotional, as usual, and when I looked up, they were all holding up heart and hand emojis in the air. Then, they slowly started to stand. They were clapping, and many of them had tears in their eyes, too. Wow. Thank you, God. May I never take that feeling for granted, and may You always bring the right people to these events.

Sometimes, people at these events are going through things you don't even know about until later. Lisa attended Wilshire Live in September of 2023. She was battling cancer at the time, which I had no idea about in the moment. Here's her story.

_____

LISA S.'S STORY

When I bought a ticket for Wilshire Live, I had no clue I was going to get diagnosed with cancer, so when I did, I wasn't sure if I would be able to attend since I was in between surgeries. I asked my doctor, and he said, "Yes, go to Nashville and enjoy yourself." I had such a great time at

Wilshire Live, as well as visiting with my sister, whom I don't see often since we don't live close.

It was just what I needed at a very scary time. After attending the live event, my sister messaged Stacey in October to tell her my story. At that time, I had just had my second surgery after a cancer diagnosis and was headed for radiation next.

She not only shared with me that she had sent the message, but she also shared with me Stacey's reply and her offers for prayers and support. I fought hard and made it through, and I truly feel the prayers and good thoughts from you and many other friends and family were responsible for getting me through it. Today, I can happily say I've been almost two years with no evidence of disease.

My sister did not attend Wilshire Live 2023, but because I always talk about Wilshire and Stacey, she decided to attend Wilshire Live 2025 with me. She enjoyed herself so much that she's attending Wilshire Live 2026 with me again. I'm grateful to have found you all those years ago, and you're helping me cope with my situation.

———

The next event was in 2025 for around seventy-five ladies from over twenty states, and it was pure magic. This is where I also had that full-circle moment.

Remember those holiday shows Blair and I used to do at that beautiful barn venue? Yep, that's where I hosted my 2025 event. To think I went from being a vendor to then hosting an event there was truly special to me.

This was another all-hands-on-deck effort from my team and event planner, and I couldn't do these big events without them. Kellie and I both had some major setbacks, health struggles, and surgeries at the beginning of 2025 (more on that to come). But together, and with the help of Kendra, the event planner, and the rest of the team, we were still able to pull it off.

This was our first Connect and Create event, and we did just that. We kicked it off with our Connect kickoff party. The ladies shopped until they dropped, and then I got to host a dinner party for seventy-five of my closest friends, something I'll never forget.

One of my favorite parts of these events is the moment the doors open. The excitement is through the roof for all of us. That's when they come in, grab their swag, and usually head straight to the photo booth. This is the moment where I get to hug their necks and see their faces.

Some are coming for the first time, and some for the second, third, or even fourth time. One of the most emotional moments of this event was seeing Melanie D. in line for the photo booth.

I knew her name, but I didn't know her face; we had never met in person. But we'd had a connection prior to the event. I looked up and saw a lady with tears in her eyes, and then I saw her name tag: Melanie D. I immediately knew who she was.

We hugged and sobbed. Her sister, who was with her, was crying as well. Melanie told me in that moment that I had helped save her, and I had no idea the impact I'd had on her life.

I didn't need to know more.

I knew she would share more when she was ready. Instead, I just hugged her and told her how thankful I was that she was there and that I could help her in any way. I'm so glad that Melanie decided to share more of her story, because it's one I'll never forget.

———

MELANIE D.'S STORY

I found Stacey and Wilshire Collections in 2021. I had recently found the crafting community on Facebook, and several I followed would mention her and how much they liked following her for craft ideas and decorating. I still remember the first live show I watched.

It was a Christmas in July edition. I was instantly hooked. I love the craft, but more than that, I felt a connection.

She had a way of connecting with her audience. I watched the Lives, the Christmas tree decorating, the Christmas craft events, all the things. Shortly after, I joined the Printable Club and the Decorating and Creating Community.

They all became my friends. There was such a connection. We laughed together, cried together, and prayed for each other.

There was a Wilshire Live event coming up, and I really wanted to go, but it just wasn't in the cards for me that year. I knew maybe one day I would have a chance. In December 2022, we were on a DC Live.

When we went online that day, I asked the group to please pray for my husband. He was very sick but didn't quite have a diagnosis yet. Of course, many mentioned they would pray for us.

This was more than just a group of crafters. It was a family that comes together when times get hard. After that Facebook Live, Stacey reached out to me, as she knew that I was pretty upset and my husband wasn't doing well.

Even with everything going on in her life, she wanted to know what she could do for me and how she could help me. To be honest, I was over-whelmed by her kindness and generosity. From that time forward, there was a bond between us.

In January 2023, my husband passed away. My community was there for me. You see, we were all online friends.

I didn't live close to any of them, nor had I ever met them, but they were my friends. They encouraged me and prayed for me. I'll always remember the kindness that was shown to me.

I was determined to get tickets for my sister and me to attend the Wilshire Live event in April 2025. The first person we met in line was Alice Ann. I recognized her name from the online DC Lives.

We began talking with her and discovered we had so much in common. I'll be forever grateful for a newfound friend. We now text each other and talk occasionally on the phone.

It was time for the event to begin. We made our way inside and were greeted by Stacey's amazing team. Everyone was so nice and welcoming.

We stood in line at the photo booth to meet Stacey. This was very overwhelming and emotional. She was someone that I met online, but I felt like I really knew her, and she knew me.

I know that God had a plan for me the whole time. He knew how much support I would need after my husband passed. He gave me the most amazing community of friends that I had only met online but now have met in person.

Fast forward, I bought my ticket to the next Wilshire event in 2026, and I can't wait to see them all again. Isn't it amazing how one small act of kindness, one message, one check-in, one "just thinking of you" can change so much? Sometimes we underestimate how much those moments matter.

———

To me, reaching out to Melanie felt simple, natural, just what you do when someone's struggling. But to her, it was a lifeline. It reminded me that God often uses our ordinary gestures to do His extraordinary work.

Reach out when people are hurting. Be a friend when someone needs a friend. Go the extra mile, even when it feels small, because you never know how far that love might travel.

I love seeing the families that come to events. We have mother–daughter combos that always show up, which is so cute. Some people bring their sister or another crafty friend.

And while many people do come with others, we also have so many who come alone to these events. I recognize how scary that can feel, and it makes me so proud when women are brave enough to do that. I always try to reassure them that the moment they arrive, I promise they won't be alone anymore. We make it our mission to be sure everyone feels included and that everyone makes connections.

In 2025, we gave our battles over to God as an activity at the event. We wrote down something we wanted to release to Him. It was *so* powerful and moving. As the women took some time to write down what they wanted to hand over to God, they came up and "released it" by putting it in a basket. There were tears, hugs, and silent prayers throughout the room. These are the moments at events like this that make them even more special than they already are.

> As I hope you can see, these events aren't about the crafts, and they certainly aren't about me. They are about something so much bigger. They're about making friendships and being surrounded by a group of women who all share a common love. They're about taking time for you, treating yourself, and having your cup filled.

In April of 2026, I will host my next in-person event. Thank you, God, for giving me the platform to be able to facilitate gatherings like this.

I have no doubt that He is once again sending all the women to this event who need it the most. I have no doubt it will be pure magic. Friends will get to reunite, go to dinner, shop together outside of the event hours, stay at houses and hotels together, and so much more.

I have no doubt that some will come alone and scared. Some will come with heartache and hurt, looking for something more. I have no doubt we will connect, create, and make cute things once again.

But more than anything, I have no doubt that this will continue to be *bigger*.

CHAPTER 5
FINDING AN OUTLET THROUGH CREATIVITY

This journey of mine took another huge pivot in 2020 when the world shut down. I went into that year so hopeful, picking the word *believe* as my word of the year.

I was starting to believe in myself and in my purpose for the first time ever, but I never could have guessed just how much I would have to trust and believe that year. When everything happened in March of 2020, I can remember feeling paralyzed in my business. *How am I supposed to show up and spread joy when I'm worried, hurting, scared, and unable to go out?* I wondered. *How am I supposed to act like nothing's wrong when there is so much uncertainty in our country, and people are dying and suffering? Will people think I don't care about what's going on if I'm Live crafting and decorating?* All of it felt so trivial in that moment.

I felt stuck, and other friends in my space felt the same way. One day, I did what I knew to do: I popped on camera Live to be real and vulnerable. I told them how I was feeling, how I didn't know what this was going to look like for me, how I didn't know if I *could* show up with everything that was going on in the world.

And their response was overwhelming. They needed me to show up. They wanted an escape from reality, and they craved creativity and connection in a time when everyone felt so lonely.

The joy I had been spreading all these years didn't need to stop because of COVID. In fact, it needed to show up more than ever before. So I showed up, and for that hour or so that I was Live each time, it was like the world stopped.

It felt like we were normal again. We could laugh and create cute things. And if we needed to, we could cry together, too.

We were walking through the emotions in real time. I didn't have to pretend everything was okay. Instead, I brought real emotions and let people know it was okay *not* to be okay.

I let them know it was also okay to laugh, to have fun, and to keep living life as best we could. Sometimes, it isn't about having all the answers. It's about showing up with honesty and heart, even when you're unsure yourself.

Here's what I didn't expect: group therapy. Creativity became a form of therapy for both me and my community. Even though we were miles apart, the glue guns and laughter connected us.

For a little while, it didn't feel like we were just crafting; we were healing together. It became an outlet for us all. Angela's story is a great example of this.

———

ANGELA R.'S STORY

I really started watching Stacey during the winter when COVID hit. I had recently lost a job that I probably would have retired from. I felt very lost, bored, and uncertain about everything that was going on in our world with the shutdown due to COVID.

The youngest of my three children had just graduated from college and moved away. I didn't know how to handle being an empty nester and really felt as though I had no real purpose in life anymore. I was lost and lonely. I had to recreate my life and find my own life and hobbies. My life has always revolved around my children.

I just started throwing myself into my home. I'd always been into decorating and crafting and had always been told I had a knack for it. I found myself looking forward to your Lives and looking at all your decorating sites. I just threw myself into decorating my home and shopping for it.

I couldn't believe I actually found a community of women just like me. I love the decor ideas, the chats, the shopping halls, and especially when you give your home tours. Between watching the Live shopping and decorating my home for everyday and especially holidays, I found a way to find joy in decorating and connecting with other women with the same passion, and it helped me get through one of the most painful times in my life.

It became an outlet for me. You don't even begin to know how much what you do helps people. So many of us are struggling through hard times in our lives, and just hearing and seeing someone who we can relate to and share a hobby with really can brighten our day and soul.

Shopping and making our homes beautiful is really a form of therapy. I'm so grateful I found this site and community during COVID and during that hard time.

PAT P.'S STORY

I really am not one to follow people on Facebook, but when my daughter was graduating from high school, I decided my house needed an update. I was drawn to Stacey because she showed how to pull it all together... craft and decorating. Her home was a lot like mine, and I could see how small changes made a big difference. In the end, my entire house was transformed.

I became more inspired... even attended the first live event and sat in the front row. I had a blast... I loved how she opened her heart to all of us, how her family supported her, and how real she is. I met so many great friends and felt right at home!

And then came Covid… it seems unreal now, but it was a very scary and uncertain time for everyone! Thank God I joined the DC when it was first introduced! For me, it became the place I could go… feel like I was with my decorating family… get inspired… but at the same time keep things real. We all came together during that time even more than before.

We definitely had new things to deal with… how to get supplies during Covid for her crafts, what possible substitutes we could use, etc. She created Zoom craft nights so we could talk and share while crafting and still be connected. But most importantly… she shared her own heart and opened the group up to share theirs. Without realizing it… the DC calendar became one of the most important outside connections and outlets for me.

———

I hope I gave others like Angela and Pat permission to breathe, to laugh, to find passions, and to find light in the small things again. When the world felt so heavy, creating something beautiful reminded us that joy still exists.

Everything we did together became a little piece of hope. Distractions are not a bad thing, and they certainly don't mean you don't care.

> Distractions are something that keep your mind focused on the good left in the world instead of what's falling apart around you.

These days that we had together didn't feel like we were just on Facebook. They felt like gatherings, a modern-day version of women sitting around the table crafting together, only this stretched across the country. And the more I showed up, the more other people did too.

We would have real conversations. They would share about people they knew who were battling COVID, we would talk about our fears, and so much more. It brought a sense of belonging and togetherness.

I can remember, after days and days of not leaving my house, I would be like, "I'm headed to the craft room to go Live. I need my ladies right now." I needed that connection and outlet just as much as they did.

So many were at home, either not working or working from home. I began to see my following grow, more people showing up to my Lives, more engagement, more community building, more sales.

My business was growing faster than it ever had before, something I did not see coming in such a hard and dark time in the world. When the world shut down, God opened new doors for connection. I embraced it and realized that not only were people craving connection, but they were looking for that outlet.

So many ladies have told me how they had crafted or decorated when they were younger, but it got put on hold because of having kids or a career. Those COVID years had them dusting off their craft supplies and finding that love again. People were looking for projects to do, and I was there to give them ideas and inspiration and hopefully some laughs along the way.

I truly feel that 2020 and 2021 brought us all so much closer, and as strange as it is to say, I'm thankful that time period brought us this. I thought that year might break my business when COVID first started, but instead, it built my faith and my business side by side.

It was during this time that I had a major breakthrough in my business. This breakthrough didn't come when things were easy. It came when I was exhausted, unsure, and wondering how I would proceed with everything going on.

Remember how I told you about the breakdown I had in 2019, when I told Anthony I would go get a job at Kirkland's if I couldn't make this work? Let me explain that more. From the outside looking in, I'm sure people thought I had a very successful business at that time. But it was costing me a lot of money to run the business, and while it was a profitable business at that time, it wasn't thriving and growing in the way I'd hoped, considering all the work I was putting in.

I truly felt it inside me that something big was coming; I just didn't know what that would look like. Then, when COVID first started, I thought, *Well, this is it. This is the end of my business. This is going to be what breaks me.* But something was coming that no one could have prepared me for.

> Sometimes our biggest breakthroughs come right after our breakdowns.

God saw and knew that I was standing on the edge of something new by showing up so often for my community during that time. I'm talking about my *"aha"* lightbulb crafting moment and how it totally changed my life and my business.

I had designed a few printables over the years that I put on my blog for people to print and put in picture frames. And one day it hit me: if scrapbook paper is paper, and you can craft with scrapbook paper, and printables are paper, why couldn't you craft with a printable? So I grabbed a Dollar Tree surface, slapped a printable on there with some Mod Podge, and the light bulb went off.

You can craft with printables. And oh my Lanta, did this take off fast in the crafting community. My community quickly became as obsessed as I was, and I started designing and selling printables in May of 2020.

By August of that year, I was launching the Printable Club because my community was asking me to turn this into a monthly thing where they could get these all the time. The Printable Club is a digital subscription that includes six digital printable bundles each month that subscribers can print and frame or get crafty with. It took off like wildfire and changed the entire trajectory of my life and business.

To my surprise, 800 ladies from my community joined the Printable Club when I first opened the doors that year, and since then, thousands more have joined over the years.

That moment from 2019 where I had told Anthony I was on the verge of a breakthrough, well, that was my breakthrough. That was when I knew I could make this work long-term.

Please note that this was seven years into my business. Seven years of hustling, pivoting, wins, and failures. Seven years of pouring into this business without seeing a whole lot in return to speak of. There were so many times over those seven years when I thought about throwing in the towel.

When I was at my lowest, struggling with my health problems, depression, and feeling like I was working hard for hardly anything, God said, "Keep going. I've got you." And He did. That light bulb moment wasn't just creativity; it was clarity. God planted an idea in my head that changed everything.

What looked like a simple craft became the spark of something that would reach thousands of women. Wow. Only God. I used to think faith and business were two separate things, but now I know they grow best together.

God didn't just build my business that year; He continued to build me. Between my health struggles that started in 2017, all the way through one of the scariest times in our world in 2020, He was shaping me and giving me a testimony for others to see. The Printable Club is still going strong five years later, and it's an absolute joy and pleasure to design seasonal and everyday printables each month for the PC girls.

Tonya M. was one of the many who found me during COVID and during the start of the printables, and this is what she had to say.

———

TONYA M.'S STORY

I first came across Stacey on Facebook during the COVID days. When I started watching her, I realized her decorating style was something I truly loved and wanted to bring into my own home. When she launched the Printable Club, I joined in and started creating projects for my space.

Honestly, I didn't think I had a creative bone in my body until then. As she shared new ways to decorate, I found myself using her ideas to make my home beautiful. Everything started to coordinate, and I fell in love with making my home feel special.

At a time like that in the world, Stacey was an outlet and an inspiration to me and my decorating journey, and I'm so thankful for everything she shares and teaches me still to this day.

———

I would venture to say that a big portion of my super-loyal following found me during those COVID years.

And not only that, but some of them found themselves during that time as well. They found a love and passion that had either been buried deep down or never revealed, and that is super special.

Here's the thing, and the theme once again with me going all in after that aha moment: I wasn't a graphic designer. I didn't even have a ton of experience designing printables, but I did it scared and knew I could learn and grow in my skills, so that's exactly what I did. I may not have believed I had the skills to do this, but I believed in God's timing, His provision, and the idea that He had placed on my heart.

So I did what I always do, and I did it scared. The years and years of printables have brought so much joy to so many lives and so much cuteness to so many homes. It's an honor to see all the cute things that PC girls make every month with their printables.

So many women love it because it's easy. You don't need to have any fancy equipment like a Cricut in order to use a printable. You can have quick-win projects done within minutes that look like they came from your favorite home decor store. It truly was (and still is) a game-changer in crafting and decorating.

And many ladies also sell the cute decor pieces they make, since they have the commercial rights to do so with their membership. What is a blessing to me is now a blessing to others and their businesses, which I love. When I asked the PC girls what being in the Printable Club meant to them, this is a summary of what they said.

Every month feels like Christmas morning when the new printables come out. They wait in anticipation for those new designs to drop. And when they do, it's like opening a present made just for them.

There's always something for everyone, and they love the versatility of them. They love that they can frame them, craft with them, turn them into cards, gifts, etc. For so many of them, Printable Club has made decorating affordable and fun again.

No more expensive art or cluttered storage bins, just easy-to-swap designs that make their homes feel cozy, seasonal, and joyful all year.

The best compliment they gave me, though, was how this club has given them confidence. Some of them never thought they were crafty until they found the printables and realized how simple and enjoyable it was to create with them.

They said it wasn't just about decor; it was about joy and inspiration. It's that excitement of knowing each month they get to be creative again and make their homes unique and special.

And that's what it's all about. The Printable Club isn't just a subscription; it's a monthly spark of creativity and joy. It's a reason to slow down, pull out your scissors and Mod Podge, and do something just for you.

These ladies don't just download printables. They share ideas, encourage one another, and celebrate their creations together. It's a space where confidence blooms and where so many women who were once scared to start because they didn't feel creative can now proudly share their projects and say, "Look what I made."

When I think about the Printable Club, I can't help but smile. What started as a simple aha moment idea has turned into something far bigger than I ever imagined. For me, the Printable Club is a reflection of everything I love about this community: creativity, connection, encouragement, and joy. It's women from all over creating something beautiful with their own two hands. It's the messages I get from ladies who tell me that they hadn't crafted in years until they joined, or, *"I didn't think I was creative and crafty until I started using printables."* It's the laughter during the Facebook Lives when I'm giving them ideas on how to use them, the proud photo shares, and the way everyone cheers each other on. It's watching women go from *"I could never do that,"* to *"Look at what I made,"* and realizing that confidence is one of the most beautiful things we can create.

The Printable Club reminds me every single month that this club was never just about the papers they print. It's about the people behind the paper. It's about bringing joy to ordinary days and helping women rediscover their creative spark. So every time I design a new bundle, I don't just see a printable. I see the faces of these women who will turn it into something special, who will hang it in their homes with pride, gift it to a friend, craft with their kids or grandkids, or even be able to make money from selling the crafts they make with them.

That is what keeps me inspired month after month. The Printable Club is a little piece of my heart shared with all of you. And the fact that it's become such a meaningful part of your lives, well, that's the greatest gift of all.

For so many, using the printables during COVID became an emotional outlet, a little slice of happiness in an unsettling time. But here we are, on the other side of those initial COVID years, and the outlet of happiness remains. Looking back, I see now that 2020 wasn't just the year of the printable for my business. It was the year of the possible.

When I thought everything was falling apart, God was actually rearranging the pieces into something better.

Every printable I designed, every Live I did, and every scared step I took was building not just a business, but a purpose. That season taught me that faith doesn't always look like giant leaps.

And those printables and Live sessions I gave people during COVID were an outlet for me, too. They were a creative escape and moments of joy in such a dark time. I'll never be able to thank my community enough for how they helped *me* get through that time emotionally.

Did I expect my business to grow in such a hard time for our world? Absolutely not. But I kept showing up, kept being faithful, and kept doing it scared. Some days, it looked like small, steady steps with Mod Podge in one hand and trust in the other.

So many other things were happening right alongside the printable craze and this time of growth. My social media following was growing, my blog was getting more views than ever before, and what had seemed like such a slow and steady race since 2013 suddenly went into turbo speed. Over those next couple of years, I was selling out of mystery decor boxes and anything else I put out there, sometimes literally within minutes. I was collaborating with other businesses, like the launch of Infinity Frames, which I partnered on with Marissa S. of Sayers and Co., and it became a fast-and-furious hit.

My business was growing, and so were my gray hairs. It was great, but it was a lot all at once. I was learning how to navigate it all and finally decided it was time to truly invest in myself and my business if I wanted to continue to grow, and grow in a way that made sense. I took a big plunge and joined my first Mastermind. Those years helped shape me, taught me so much, and showed me that I'm worth investing in. They also led me to some of my best business friends that I still have to this day.

A lot happened in my business in just a couple of years, from the start of COVID through 2022, and it truly changed my life… and my family's lives. And in turn, all I've been able to do is change so many of yours for the better as well. That is something I will forever be grateful for.

While I never want to go back to a time like those COVID years, I sure did learn and grow a lot. In the beginning, if you had told me that something beautiful could grow out of that time, I wouldn't have believed you.

But God used those years to knit our community tighter than ever before. And He knew all along that even in this season of life… *it was bigger*.

CHAPTER 6
DOING IT SCARED

I told you how scared I was to hit that "Go Live" button back in the day. That girl with no self-esteem, health struggles, and true fear sat at her kitchen table and did it anyway.

She did it scared. At this point in my journey, my community was growing, my subscriptions were growing, my confidence was growing, my team was growing, and my faith was growing. None of it happened overnight, though, and every single bit of it took hard work, late nights, tears, and more than a few "Lord, are you sure about this?" prayers.

As Wilshire kept expanding, so did the need for more hands and hearts to help me carry the vision. With each person I brought onto my team, the fear crept in.

Will they be a good fit?

Will I have enough work for them to do?

Do I know how to be a leader?

But I had to do it.

As time went on, things were growing, and it became too much to handle for just Caity and me. We were a team of two doing the work of many. Little did I know that as each person came along to Team Wilshire, we were slowly building something together even more special than I could have imagined.

First came Caity, my project manager. Caity takes all my ideas and visions and brings them to life in such a beautiful way with all the tech things that are needed, like sales pages, spreadsheets, automations, and more. She may be more behind the scenes, but she keeps things ticking smoothly so I can focus on the creative side of the business, which is so important.

Then came Amanda, my customer support manager. Amanda does customer service and website support. She's someone who loves our community just as much as I do and helps take care of our people with such grace and kindness. If you've ever emailed support, chances are you were talking to her, and I have no doubt she helped you in a loving and patient way.

Then came Kellie, my local creative manager, who is my right-hand gal on the daily. Kellie helps bring ideas and creativity to everything we do by planning, prepping, brainstorming, and more. I call her my "emotional support human." I'm joking, but it's also true. Many of the ladies have gotten to know her from her presence on many of my Facebook Lives, and I have no doubt she loves this community as much as I do.

And then came Lacey, my marketing manager, the behind-the-scenes glue that helps me make all the content and marketing magic happen. From her creative ideas to email and social strategies and so much more, she's always up to any task. She's there with a helping hand to take stress off my plate with a shared goal to thrive, grow, and love on our community, something that simply can't be done alone.

These girls (the Dream Team) are the heartbeat of Wilshire, and I don't take for granted for a second how blessed I am to have them. I know my community feels the same way about them, especially those who have had the privilege to meet them at my live events. Each of them was referred to me by someone I've known along the way, and I truly feel like that word-of-mouth reference has made all the difference in bringing on the right people.

There are so many others who help me in my business, from Ryan, Dan, and the fulfillment center team to my amazing sourcing expert Marissa, to extra website and tech support from Mat, to keeping my books and taxes in order from Corissa, and so much more. It truly takes a village.

One person who may not be on the team on paper but is crucial to my business is Anthony, my husband. He hears and sees it all, and he's been by my side every step of the way: when I was excited and just starting; when I was at rock bottom wanting to quit; when I was growing faster than I could handle; and when I brought each new idea to him with pride. He's held me while I cried, he's laughed with me through it all, and he's never once questioned my why or made me feel like I couldn't do everything I set out to do. That, my friends, is love, true and unconditional love, and I'll never be able to thank him enough.

All that to say, when I started this business, I never set out to be a boss. I still don't love that word, and my team will tell you that, but somehow, that's exactly where God led me. I found myself leading, mentoring, and building something so much bigger than I ever thought possible.

Was I scared every time I brought someone new on board? 100 percent. Bringing people into your business means trusting them with your dream, but I learned that growth often requires surrender, trusting God, and trusting others. It also requires releasing control, which is something that is hard for me to do.

Have there been challenges along the way? Of course. Other team members have come and gone, and I've had to learn to navigate leadership through both the highs and the hard seasons. But every single experience taught me something about communication, about grace, about patience, and about letting people shine in their own strengths.

Being in this role as CEO, leader, and friend has stretched me in ways I never expected. I've learned that leadership isn't about having all the answers. It's about creating an environment where people feel valued, supported, and seen.

At the end of the day, I don't see myself as a boss. I see myself as a woman chasing a God-given dream, surrounded by incredible women who believe in that same vision. Together, we're not just running a business. We're building something that brings joy, connection, and creativity into the world.

And honestly, that's what makes this journey so worth it. I don't know what the future holds for the growth and expansion of the team, but I do know that God has brought the right people at the right time to me in the past, and He will continue to do so. I'll never be able to give sufficient thanks to the Dream Team, all the extra people that work alongside me, and Anthony for always supporting me with every dream and every "Hey, I have an idea" message that comes their way.

One of those "Hey, I have an idea" messages to my team happened in 2023, one no one saw coming, but that everyone supported. To fully understand it, you first need to know about my problem, I mean, passion. You see, I'm obsessed with pillows, and I always have been.

I do this thing on my page called "whisper-shopping," which is basically where I go Live in stores, but I whisper because, hello, it's super awkward to go Live in a store with people around. So whisper-shopping kind of became my thing, and people love to watch those videos, and I love to shop and do them. For years, people saw me buying pillows left and right, whispering as I shopped for the different seasons.

I truly believe that a pillow can be a starting point for a room's inspiration and can completely update and transform a space. Plus, they are just fluffy and cute. A lot of times, the pillows I would share would come from places like TJ Maxx, and oftentimes, ladies would go on a wild goose chase trying to find them. But as you probably know, not all TJ Maxx stores are created equal, so they would often get frustrated if they couldn't find the same item.

Things were cruising along really well in 2023, and I honestly didn't need another thing on my plate, and then it happened. I was getting ready in my bathroom one morning when I started thinking about how much I would love to have a line of pillows in a store one day. That's always been one of those big, scary bucket-list things for me: to have my products in a store.

Then I thought to myself, *why do I need to wait for a store when I could just do it myself and sell them myself?* But then I quickly thought, *No, who are you? You're not a pillow designer. You don't know the first thing about that or where to start.* That impostor syndrome set in once again, so I tried to squash it down. But just like a fluffy pillow, I couldn't hide it, and I could not stop thinking about it.

At first, I didn't tell a soul about this little vision I had. It was my first year in a new Mastermind, and a few weeks after that moment, I had a one-on-one call with Sarah W., who leads the Elevate Mastermind. At the very end of our call, I mentioned to her that I had one other idea, but that it would probably never happen. I shared with her my idea for creating a pillow cover I could send to ladies every month so they could swap it out and create pretty spaces. This way, we could have all the cute pillows we wanted but not have to stress over where to store the big, bulky ones. I also knew there was a need for high-quality, adorable pillow covers.

When I told Sarah this idea, she told me not only that it was going to happen, but that it needed to happen now. She knew I was onto something and that it was the perfect fit for my audience and my business. We immediately started brainstorming how I could make this happen. This is exactly why it's so important to be connected in business. I didn't have all the answers, but Sarah had some connections and ideas.

One of my biggest obstacles with it was discovering over the years that shipping does not bring me joy, and I knew I simply wasn't up for shipping that kind of volume from my house. In the Nashville area, it's very expensive to rent warehouse space, and that honestly was not a goal or dream of mine anyway. So Sarah introduced me to a fulfillment center that specializes in shipping subscription boxes for businesses just like mine. I had no idea that something like that existed. It seemed like the perfect solution to that obstacle.

I didn't know the first thing about sewing or a flange or embroidery or any of it. I truly had to learn as I went, but I was lucky to have an amazing sourcing expert, Marissa S., helping me. She found the perfect manufacturer for my needs, and I couldn't have done it all without her help. The same manufacturer that makes my pillows makes pillows for stores like Kirkland's, TJ Maxx, At Home, and more. Who would have ever dreamed that would happen? Not me, for sure.

When I told my team and Anthony that I'd had another new idea, I remember thinking, *Oh my gosh, are they gonna all run for the hills?* Guess what? No one ran. Instead, they were all so excited and supportive and said, "Let's do it. How do we make it happen?"

Again, I was doing it before I was ready, and I was doing it scared, but fear was not going to hold me back from this dream. Looking back, I see how God planted this seed years earlier. Every time I picked up a pillow on a "whisper-shopping" trip, He was whispering a little dream in my heart.

> Every new chapter starts with a little bit of fear and a whole lot of faith. And if I've learned anything through this journey, it's that courage doesn't mean you aren't scared; it means you do it anyway.

I can't tell you how many times I've sat on the edge of a new idea with my heart pounding, thinking, *Who am I to do this? What if I fail? And what if no one cares?* Every single big moment in my business has come with fear sitting right beside me.

But do you know what else was sitting beside me? Faith. Because here's the honest truth: I've never once felt ready. Not when I painted that first piece of furniture, not when I hit "Go Live" for the first time, not when I started the DC, not when I started the PC, and definitely not when this pillow dream was laid on my heart. I just felt a little nudge from God saying, "Trust me." And so I did it scared.

There's a saying I love:

God doesn't call the qualified; He qualifies the called.

And that's been the story of my life. He's taken this Southern girl with a paintbrush, a laptop, and a whole lot of dreams and used it for something so much bigger. He can do the same for you.

I'm not special. I wasn't handed anything on a silver platter. I've just been obedient, and I've worked really, really hard.

God doesn't wait until we're ready. He just asks us to take the leap because faith isn't the absence of fear. It's moving forward in spite of it and trusting that He already has your path laid out for you.

If you wait until you're ready or until the timing is perfect, chances are that day will not come, and it will never happen. You have to trust. So in August of 2023, I did just that.

That August, the Pillow Cover Club was born and was a huge hit right out of the gate.

I had built up a lot of excitement with making the community guess what was up next, doing countdowns, and engaging in other hype-building techniques. By the time I was ready to launch, people were excited for this next adventure.

It was actually happening. I was now a pillow designer and was embarking on a journey that I truly didn't know much about at the time, but I knew I had a passion, a purpose, and a vision for what this club could be. And I trusted that God would help me with the rest. Now, two-plus years later, I still design and ship pillow covers for all the seasons and reasons to ladies all across the country. I call them my "Pillow Besties."

One thing I've learned by teaching women how to decorate is that not everyone has confidence in their decorating or DIY skills. In fact, most feel like they need help in one way or another with those areas, which is why they come to me in the first place. I encourage them that they don't have to know it all. They don't have to be experts. They just have to start. And the times I've seen people do just that, over and over again, are so amazing.

I've also found that people find me when they're at some kind of crossroad in their life, and they need an outlet. And when they find it, they jump in feet first without knowing what to expect, but they are doing it scared anyway.

LaShae B.'s story is a great example of just that.

———

LASHAE B.'S STORY

In May 2024, I retired after thirty-three wonderful years in education.

My husband had already retired after thirty-seven years in education himself. For so long, our lives revolved around school activities, events, and constant motion. So when we both retired, I found myself unsure of what to do with the free time.

Out of boredom, I began scrolling Facebook, something I wasn't very familiar with. At the time, I kept seeing posts from Wilshire Collections. Your name kept popping up, and I became more and more intrigued by your videos and decorating tips.

There was something so warming and genuine about you that I couldn't wait until your next Live. In November 2024, I took a leap and joined the Pillow Cover Club. When I received my first pillow, I was completely hooked.

I always thought I was an okay decorator, but you've helped me grow so much in my confidence and creativity. Then I heard you talking about the Decorating and Creating Community, and I knew I had to be a part of it too. I was jumping in feet first and immediately fell in love with the group.

I love how real, raw, and vulnerable you are with us, and your loving compassion for people is so evident. We laugh, we cry, we create, and it truly feels like a family. You're such a light, and your heart for others shines so brightly. I always say you're like an extension cord of Jesus, spreading joy, connection, and creativity wherever you go.

The final club I joined was the Printable Club, and wow, what a game-changer. Being able to coordinate pillows, crafts, and printables made decorating so much easier and so much more enjoyable. Everything just works together and takes all the guesswork out of it.

Wilshire Collections has truly changed my life. What began as boredom during retirement turned into me taking a leap when I saw those videos pop up and led me on a beautiful journey of rediscovering purpose, joy, and community.

I'm so grateful to be a part of something so special, and I wanna thank you from the bottom of my heart.

————

Linda V. has a similar story.

LINDA V.'S STORY

I was at a point in my life when, upon retirement, I had an emptiness of sorts that needed to be filled. Then one day, I discovered Wilshire Collections. I started watching your Lives and watching you share your gift for decorating and creating. Your genuine caring and kindness towards all your followers, and realizing you're a woman of faith, made me feel like I had found the thing I had been seeking to fill the void.

Beyond the inspirational decorating, creativity, and humor, you share your faith through creating a monthly prayer thread, as well as your Sunday messages. I believe God leads us to unexpected places and shows us unexpected opportunities in our life journey. Wilshire Collections and the DC is one of those unexpected places and unexpected opportunities that not only has encouraged me to get back into the crafting and decorating I had done so much of when I was younger, but has also given me a sense of belonging to a very special community. This community of encouragement and support is a very special place, and I'm thankful and grateful to have been given the opportunity to be part of it.

I thank you for opening up your heart to so many of us who, like you, believe God has a plan for each of us and that God is in our story.

—————

Wow, I love the idea of unexpected opportunities that we didn't see coming, but when they come, we dive in and let God do the rest.

Pillow Cover Club was one of those unexpected opportunities that I didn't see coming. This doesn't mean that every time we take those leaps, it's going to be easy or that there won't be challenges. I would be lying if I didn't tell you that the Pillow Cover Club has been my biggest undertaking yet.

There have been late nights, tears, mistakes made, self-doubt, and so much more that has happened behind the scenes. Turns out there's been a lot more to learn about this than I ever dreamed. But through this learning curve, I have grown so much too. I wouldn't trade any of it, because at the end of the day, it's the joy I see on the Pillow Besties' faces that makes it all worth it.

When I see their selfies come in and how excited they are to grab that little plaid and polka dot bag off their porches, it's just the cutest. And then when I get to see the pillows on their couches, chairs, and styled in baskets, I smile from ear to ear. When they tell me how it has helped up their decorating game, made their lives easier, helped with storage, and so much more, it truly makes every late night and every stressor that has come with it worth it.

Here's a summary of what the Pillow Besties said when I asked them what being in the Pillow Cover Club meant to them.

For them, it's more than just getting a new pillow cover every month. It's a little burst of happiness that comes right to their door.

That plaid and polka dot bag is joy delivered. Every month, they look forward to that moment, tearing open the bag to see what new design

I've dreamed up. Then they rush to swap it out on their couch, chair, bed, or basket.

It's become a ritual that makes their homes feel fresh and filled with love. The Pillow Cover Club makes decorating simple. No more overflowing closets or stress to search high and low in stores for that perfect pillow.

One new piece that can tie a whole room together, just like that. It helps them feel proud of their homes, confident in their style, and excited to show off their spaces to their family and friends. But deeper than that, it's a connection.

The ladies love sharing their pillow selfies, seeing how others style theirs, and cheering one another on. It's a community wrapped up in the shape of a pillow. For many, that monthly delivery is also a reminder to slow down and savor life's little blessings.

It's a spark of encouragement, a piece of happiness, and a tangible sign of the love, care, and creativity that I pour into everything I do.

Thank you, God, for guiding me through such a big challenge so that these ladies can gain confidence and be proud of their homes.

Thank you to every person who became a part of this journey with me: my family and team for their support to make it happen and bring these visions to life, Sarah with her bold encouragement, Marissa with her expertise, the fulfillment center for getting them out the door safely each month, and my Mastermind girls for cheering me on every step of the way. They were all placed there on purpose. God knew I needed each one of them to bring this dream to life.

It reminded me again that we aren't called to do big things alone. It takes a village. It took people believing in me, and then, of course, my community who trusted me to tackle this adventure. They showed up and showed up big when I launched this new adventure, just like they always do.

One of the biggest blessings in my business journey has been finding my people: the ones who get it, the ones who understand what it's like to have big dreams, messy middle moments, and a heart that's both scared and excited at the same time. Having business friends has been life-giving.

These are the women who cheer me on when things are going great and remind me of my purpose when things get hard. They're the ones who will pray with me before a big launch, talk me off a ledge when I'm doubting myself, and celebrate every little win like it's the Super Bowl. Surrounding yourself with people who are also doing it scared, who get it, who share your values, your work ethic, and your heart, changes everything.

They challenge you to grow. They lift you up when you fall. And they remind you that you're not crazy for chasing something that God placed on your heart. Because here's the truth: you can't pour into others if your own cup is empty. Having people who understand your world helps refill that cup. Not everyone in your everyday life will understand what you're doing or why you're doing it, and that's okay. They don't have to.

But the ones who *do* get it will be there to inspire, encourage, and keep you grounded when the noise of comparison or burnout starts to creep in. It's so important to find your people, the ones who speak truth, share your faith, and push you toward the version of yourself God created you to be. How blessed am I to have so many friends like this, both in the online space and in my real, everyday life?

I know each of them reading this knows who they are, and each of you is the woman whom I simply couldn't do life and business without. Sarah, who runs the Mastermind I'm in, has been an amazing coach and mentor to me, and I reached out to her to see if she would send a little story for the book about that day I brought the Pillow Cover Club idea to her.

She had no idea what chapter it was going to go in, what the theme of the chapter was, et cetera. So when I saw what she wrote, I got absolute chills. Read her story, and you'll see why.

SARAH W.'S STORY

I still remember the day Stacey first told me about her idea for creating her own line of pillow covers. We were on one of our Mastermind calls running through her list of questions, and then her eyes lit up when she started sharing her vision.

I could immediately see the potential, not just for a product, but for a movement within her already loyal community. My mind instantly went to how we could turn this into a recurring subscription that would let her serve her people month after month while keeping things manageable behind the scenes. At first she said, "But I don't want to ship them."

This was her biggest roadblock, but we worked through it together, found a fulfillment center, and suddenly, the things that felt impossible became completely doable. From there, she built her plan, started working on sourcing, trusted the process, and launched. The rest is history.

What inspired me the most was watching Stacey do it scared. She didn't have it all figured out, and she'll be the first to tell you that. She took a leap, even while second-guessing how many pillows to order that first month and wondering if people would buy.

But she also knew she wasn't alone. She had support, encouragement, and a community cheering her on. That combination of courage and connection is powerful, because that's what this journey is really about: doing it scared, surrounded by people who believe in you.

Stacey's story is proof that you don't have to have all the answers to start. You just have to take the first step, trust yourself, and lean on your community along the way.

———

Wow, the fact that Sarah wrote about doing it scared without knowing that that was the exact theme of this chapter is truly incredible and speaks to the power of this story. Sometimes God gives you a dream that feels way too big for your experience, but that's how you know it's from Him. He doesn't ask you to have it all figured out. He just asks you to start. And then He fills in the gaps with His provisions and the right people. Where God guides, He provides, and that continues to be true.

So I continue to take leaps and trust. I used to think that pillows were just pretty decor, but through this journey, God used my love for something simple to show me He can turn even the fluffiest passions into something meaningful and amazing. Some of my biggest blessings were waiting right on the other side of fear.

And every single time I've chosen faith, God has shown up in ways I never could have orchestrated on my own. And sometimes He pushes you way out of your comfort zone. There have been so many things that have come along that I've gone out of my comfort zone to share: my weight loss journey, health struggles, family worries, and more. Each time, it's scary, and it's vulnerable to put yourself out there like that.

But each time, it was about showing up scared to serve and help people, because that's what I was called to do. So now when those fears creep in, I remind myself that this isn't my story to control, it's His. My job is to keep showing up, loving on and serving my community, and keep trusting, and keep doing it scared.

> Looking back, I see that every single time I've said yes to God, it was wrapped in fear at first. Doing it scared and taking a leap has been my way of showing Him that I trust His plan more than my comfort zone. Because at the end of the day, courage doesn't mean you aren't scared.

It just means you've decided to trust God more than the voice in your head that's telling you that you can't do it, you aren't good enough, or your fear is bigger.

Do I think my fear is done? Nope, not at all. I don't think I'll ever be at a place where fear doesn't creep in from time to time. I think it's part of who I am. But I know my faith is stronger than any future fear, and that is what I will continue to have to trust.

I hope as you're reading this, you decide to do the thing that you're scared to do. Don't let fear stop you. Don't quit just because things are getting hard. If I had quit all those times I thought about doing so, I wouldn't have pushed past those fears and be where I am today. You have to keep going.

The Pillow Cover Club will always be one of my biggest leaps of faith. It taught me that dreams don't have to make sense to anyone else to be valid, and that when you trust God with the details, He'll surprise you with the outcome. From whisper-shopping to warehouse shipping, He's been guiding each step.

And every time I see one of my Pillow Besties share her joy, it's just another reminder that God can take the simplest passions and turn them into something bigger than we ever imagined. It's a reminder that the little dream I had in my bathroom while getting ready that day, well, God knew it was bigger all along.

CHAPTER 7
THE POWER OF AUTHENTICITY AND TRUST

If you haven't counted by now, that's three subscription groups that I currently have. The Decorating and Creating Community with the "DC girls" began in 2018, the Printable Club with the "PC girls" began in 2020, and the Pillow Cover Club with the "Pillow Besties" started in 2023. It's a running joke with my team that we aren't allowed to say the "S" word: no more new subscriptions, at least not right now. But never say never. We are very happy and content leaning into these three groups within my community.

Something adorable that happened along the way after subscription number two came was this: I realized that so many of them were in the DC, and then also joined the PC. I told them one day on a Live that we needed a name for people who were in both. They started throwing out their ideas, and someone suggested the "Double Dippers." We all laughed, and it just kind of stuck. When subscription number three rolled around, you guessed it, "Triple Dippers." How cute are they?

I will never take for granted that there are women who are in not one, not two, but all three of my groups. As of today, we have over 250 ladies who are Triple Dippers, which is truly amazing. When I asked some of the Double and Triple Dippers what being part of these groups means to them, here is a summary of what they said.

DOUBLE DIPPER AND TRIPLE DIPPER STORIES

For so many of the women in this community, one group simply isn't enough, because what they found here goes far beyond crafts, decor, or pillows. They found connection, encouragement, and they have a level of trust in me to know that what I deliver will be worth every penny spent.

The ladies who are part of more than one subscription are the most loyal of the loyal. They've seen every side of Wilshire, and they choose to stay because they know my heart. They know I'll show up for them honestly, share my real life, and always lead with faith and integrity.

They know that all of these groups tie together to give them the best possible experience that will bring joy to their everyday lives. Being a part of multiple groups isn't about more stuff; it's about belonging. It's about knowing that every space here, whether it's decorating, crafting, or pillows, carries that same spirit of encouragement, creativity, and love.

They've seen me laugh through mistakes, admit when things go sideways, and celebrate when God shows up bigger than I ever imagined. That transparency has built something money can't buy: their trust.

To me, the Double and Triple Dippers are living proof that…

> When you lead with authenticity, people don't just follow you; they link arms with you.

They trust your vision, they share your heart, and together they help you keep spreading joy farther than you could ever do on your own. Sally is one of my amazing Triple Dippers, and I just love her story.

———

SALLY E.'S STORY

I first saw Stacey in December of 2020 on Facebook. We were in the midst of COVID, and I had recently lost my little sister in a tragic accident. It was one of the worst times in my life. I was skimming through Facebook, trying to get my mind off the world, when I came across this sweet Southern belle named Stacey Collins. She was sitting at her dining room table doing some painting and mod podging and talking to her audience, but it was her sweet Southern draw and the kindness in her eyes that drew me in.

I was immediately hooked. I knew right then that this was where I would find peace and friendship by following her. I joined the Printable Club, and from then on, I watched every single day as she brightened my very dark days and taught me crafting and made me smile again.

She talked to everyone on the Live show like we were family. She was exactly what I needed. Her joy for life, her family, and her love of creating beautiful crafts held my interest, and I felt that for that hour I was surrounded by love.

The fun and laughter have never stopped as I watched Stacey grow into someone that people were in search of. I eventually joined the Decorating and Creating Community and finally the Pillow Cover Club, making me what we call a Triple Dipper. I had finally found my niche.

My deep sadness from losing my sister was lifted whenever I spent time with Stacey. Her devotion to God and her faith were passed right along to me, and I'll always love her for that. As the world began to slowly go back to normal, we continued to bring that joy back into our lives daily.

———

Thank you to not only the Double and Triple Dippers, but to every single person in any of my subscriptions. To every person in my online community, you are the heartbeat of Wilshire. You are important. If you've ever commented on a post, shared a video, gotten inspired, or trusted me to bring joy and beauty into your lives and homes, you are the reason I keep doing what I'm doing.

Thank you for believing in me and knowing that I'm always trying to do my best to serve you well. Thank you for not only investing in me, but in the community we've built together. All of you are what make it as special as it is.

I have to say this, though, because I don't want anyone to read this as easy or as something that was laid before me, because none of this happened overnight. This community that trusts me didn't just appear out of nowhere. It was built one post, one Live, one honest conversation at a time.

These women have trusted me with each new idea and each new subscription I've launched, and that trust is something I worked hard to earn and will never take lightly. Trust isn't just given to you from the very beginning. From the start, I made a promise to myself and to them that I would always be honest and real.

If something wasn't going great, I would share it. And if something was falling apart, I'd share that too.

> Because here's the truth: people can't connect with perfection; they connect with reality. And people buy from people they know, like, and trust.

Do they think I have cute products and ideas? I sure hope so. But they also know the heart and the mission behind it all. And this community of loyal women, who have come to know, like, and trust me, have trusted me with each subscription that has come along, and that is something I've worked hard to build.

I've built something so much deeper than a customer base. It's a sisterhood rooted in honesty, authenticity, vulnerability, and mutual respect. These ladies trust me so much that they will buy a product sight unseen, just because I say, "I promise it'll be cute."

They don't need full pictures or even sneak peeks. They just need that promise from me that I always deliver. And that is something I will promise to them over and over again.

The sight unseen side of things comes in with pre-orders. Sometimes the ladies will pre-order something like a throw blanket or a table runner without actually seeing the product. They just know it's going to be cute. And when you can show up in that authentic way, chances are you'll be met with grace when things do go south.

There was a time when a huge mishap happened with our t-shirt vendor at the time. I was on vacation with my family when it all went down. And to be honest, it completely stopped what we were doing in our tracks and caused a lot of drama, tears, and frustration.

What went down meant tons of people not getting their orders or getting incorrect orders and refunds having to be made, etc. All of this was 100 percent out of my control, but it was still my name attached to these shirts. I was so nervous to go Live and tell them what a mess this was.

I remember sitting there with my heart racing, thinking, *How do I tell them this, and what will they think?* But I went Live anyway. I looked into the camera, took a deep breath, got a little emotional, and then told them the truth.

And do you know what happened? Not one person complained. Not one person got ugly. Instead, they showed up with grace and support.

That moment changed me as a leader. It showed me that honesty builds more than trust; it builds loyalty.

> When you're honest, even when it's hard, you're showing people that you value their trust more than your pride.

When people know you're human and that your heart is in the right place, they'll stand by you through the ups and downs. And that's exactly what this community has done for me time and time again.

Whether it's a tech glitch, a shipping delay, or just a day where I'm overwhelmed and not my bubbly self, they get it. Because we've built something deeper than transactions. We've built relationships.

And here's another thing that's cool about community and trust. You tend to hear from a lot of the same loyal people in your community: the ones who show up to Lives, comment, post their pictures, etc. But the impact reaches far past just them. There are so many people I call "silent watchers." They're the people who watch, listen, and learn but don't comment much.

Some of them shop from you but don't comment. Some of them join the subscriptions, but they still stay silent. Even though those community members may be more behind the scenes, they're still getting to know and trust you all the same.

————

Shellie R.'s story is one of just that.

SHELLIE R.'S STORY

This group has made me feel part of something important, uplifting, and joyful over the past couple of years.

Stacey, your ability to make me feel like you're talking directly to me, like we've been friends forever, is a true gift. Your openness, honesty, authenticity, and humility are truly inspiring. And I thank you for that.

I don't tend to comment or put myself out there, but I wanted you to know that even those of us who just listen or watch you online and never comment are inspired by you and thankful for all that you do.

————

Shellie even wrote a poem to convey her feelings that I would like to share.

"I've got a friend I brag about, and though she knows me not,
She's the one I turn to when things get tough.
Whenever I'm in need of hope, she knows just what to do.
It doesn't seem that hard for her, for her inner light shines through.
She's got the kind of spirit that makes you feel you're loved
and lets you know that who you are is more than good enough.
Although we've never really met, and perhaps we never will,
I'll hold her friendship in my heart in the hopes that someday we
shall.
For friendship comes in many forms, and it doesn't matter how.
True friends are always there for you, and online will do for now."

This right here lets me know that continuing to be authentic and to keep building that trust is what will keep people coming back.

Whether they are super involved and active or a little bit more silent, each one matters. It's so important to me to celebrate my community and their wins, whether that's giving them a shout-out on the page for a project or a decorating job well done, or replying to their comments and complimenting what they've done. I want them to feel seen, loved, and heard.

I want them to know this is a safe place to share and open up. It's a mutual trust we are building here. And this same trust that we are building is what made people join one or more subscriptions.

It's what made them hit purchase on my site. It's what made them pre-order without seeing the products, or maybe just a sneak peek. It's because they know I will deliver top-notch products and services.

It's because they've come to know, like, and trust me. And that is, yet again, something I'll never take for granted. It's also so important to me to provide top-notch customer service, just like we had to make it right with the big shirt debacle.

We always want to do what's right. Amanda, who does customer support, knows exactly how to take care of the community. And we often go way above and beyond in order to keep people happy.

She has the patience of a saint and the ability to pour into the community in a way that's so special. I'm proud to say that we rarely get complaints about our customer service, and I know that our honesty and integrity are a big part of that.

This community was by my side as my family went on an adventure to build our dream home. It honestly felt like having thousands of my besties to celebrate with me and be there for me every step of the way. I shared so much of that process.

And honestly, it's because that trust is mutual. They trust me, and I trust them by letting them into my personal world in that way. It's a time that I'll never forget because they made it that much more special. They gave me so much support and love. And by the time we were set to close and move in, you would have thought it was closing day for all of them.

However, not everyone is always nice and kind. So I think it's important to talk about the other, not-so-glamorous parts of life and business, because I don't want you to read this and think how perfect it always is. That's far from the truth.

There've been so many times in my business that I've had to take the high road. Let me just tell you: the high road is often not the easiest one to take. It's quiet, it's lonely, it's humbling, and it's hard.

There've been times I've wanted to go Live and stand my ground, tell my side of the story, and set the record straight. Times when I felt like I've been misunderstood or misrepresented. I've typed and deleted posts more often than I can count and frequently had to hold myself back from hitting that "Go Live" button.

But every single time I'm tempted, I remind myself that this isn't what I was called to do. My community doesn't come to me for drama. They don't show up for gossip or negativity. They come for joy, creativity, encouragement, and light. They come for hope. And protecting that space is more important to me than trying to prove a point.

What's important is that I know the truth. The high road isn't about being passive or letting people walk all over you. It's about choosing peace over pride. It's about remembering that integrity lasts longer than any temporary feeling of being right.

And honestly, every time I've had to choose the high, hard road, God has honored it. Maybe not right away, and maybe not in the way I expected, but He always eventually brings me peace and clarity when I let Him fight the battles that don't deserve my energy.

Speaking of not deserving my energy, let's speak to the haters, the trolls, the unkind people. We aren't going to give them too much of our energy here, but I do have a cool story about how something so negative and rude turned into something amazing. You see, when you put yourself out there like I do, you are opening yourself up to the good, the bad, and the ugly.

I'm very lucky that I have a ton more positive support on my page than negative, but of course, that negativity is still there, and man, is it hurtful. Here's the thing about me: I wear my heart on my sleeve. I'm a people pleaser to my core, and the thought of someone not liking me or what I do will keep me up at night, even though I know deep down I'm not going to be for everyone, and I shouldn't have to be. But growing thick skin is something I've had to work very hard on, and still do to this day.

Little comments that I seem to hear over and over again are things like:

"Stop talking and get on with the project."

"You touch your hair too much."

"You talk too much."

In the beginning, I would cry and fret over comments like this. I was letting a complete stranger from the internet dictate my mood, my day, and my thoughts about myself. It's funny how one negative comment can drown out a thousand kind ones. You can hear praise all day long, but that one bit of criticism sticks like glue. I've learned that it can take a thousand positive comments to outweigh one negative comment.

A message came to my inbox one day that I'll never forget. Not only did a lady take the time to message me to tell me how annoying she thought my voice was (which I had heard before), but she had taken the time to send me voice memos imitating what I sounded like in the most hateful and exaggerated way. I was floored. I must have listened to it twenty-plus times as I cried through the pain.

Who is that hurt in their own life that they would take the time and energy to tear someone down who's out there trying to do some good in this world? At that point, I had had enough of the rude people, even though in the big scheme of things, they were few and far between. I felt the urge in this instance to go Live and share what had happened as a message to remind people to always be kind, so I did just that.

Through nerves and shaking hands, I told everyone about the message I had gotten and how it affected me. The outpouring of love and support I got was incredible. Because here's the thing: the ones watching that Live? They weren't the negative ones in the comments and in my DMs. They weren't the ones who really needed to hear it the most. But I needed *them* at that moment, and I needed the ones who did support me.

The enemy loves to use that one negative voice to make you forget the thousands of people cheering you on. But God's voice is louder than the criticism, and I knew that sitting with them in that moment was just what I needed to bring me back to that.

In telling that story when I was Live, I mentioned that she made me feel like I was Flash the Sloth from *Zootopia* when she imitated the way I was talking. They all loved how I was able to find humor in that moment, and what happened next was simply the cutest.

I started getting Happy Mail, and in that Happy Mail, sloth-themed items, from notebooks to coffee mugs to socks to little stuffed animals, the gifts came pouring in. And slowly, pun intended, the sloth became a little mascot of sorts for Wilshire. To this day, every time I see one, I can't help but smile. It reminds me of how loved and seen I was by this amazing group of women who watched me online.

They knew me and knew what I needed in that moment. And it was in that moment that I realized I can't let one bad seed make me forget the whole garden I've grown. It was at that moment that I started to work on developing a thicker skin and focusing on the good that far outweighed the bad.

Do I still get rude people, nasty comments and messages, and things that are hurtful sent my way? All the time. But I've tried to remember over the years that I can't let that one voice outweigh the thousands that know, like, and trust me and are cheering me on.

I can't let all those good comments fade to the background while the negative ones stick around, replaying in my mind like a bad song I can't turn off. Early in my business, I let those negative comments really get to me. I'd stay up late rereading them, reading them to trusted friends and family, and wondering what I could have said or done differently. And I was putting way too much focus on that.

Over the years, I've learned something about the people who leave the mean comments. While I'm far from perfect, most of the time it's not about me, it's about them. Those people are hurting. People who are happy, whole, and secure in their lives don't usually take the time to tear someone down whom they don't even know. The ones who lash out are often the ones who are battling something we can't see: pain, loneliness, insecurity, or a deep need to be seen.

So instead of getting angry or hurt, I've started doing something different. I bless them and block them. I remove them from my page and my life, and then I pray for them, I truly do. I remind myself that hurt people often hurt people, and that my job isn't to fix them or change who I am; it's to stay true to who God's called me to be.

I ask God to heal whatever hurt is hiding behind their words. And every time I choose prayer over pettiness, peace follows. I can't control what people say about me or my business, but I can control how I respond. I choose to protect my peace, my purpose, and the joy that God has given me. If I could give advice on this to anyone else, it would be to not let one negative voice make you forget the thousands of hearts you've impacted. It's not worth it.

Protect your peace, keep your eyes on your purpose, and let God handle the rest. So whether it's showing up as my real and authentic self to build that trust, or taking the high road, or protecting my peace, it's all important, and it's all shaped me into who I am today as a business owner and woman. Because every time I show up with honesty, whether it's to share a win or admit something went wrong, I'm reminded that this isn't just a business; it's a ministry of trust.

I'm so thankful that you don't just support what I do; you believe in why I do it. You've shown me that when you build something real and rooted in faith, people don't just join for the projects; they stay for the purpose. You're proof that this community is bigger than one group or one idea.

It's about connection, creativity, and a whole lot of heart. Thank you for letting me lead you, create with you, and grow alongside you. Y'all are the heartbeat of Wilshire Collections, and I'll forever be grateful for the joy you've brought into my life.

God has blessed me with this community of women who see my heart, even when things get messy. And every time I'm tempted to hide behind perfection, He gently reminds me that authenticity is where connection lives. He reminds me that what we are building here is even bigger than we could imagine.

CHAPTER 8
THE RIPPLE EFFECT

I f there's one thing I've learned through this journey, it's that when women come together with hearts full of love and faith, miracles happen. The impact of this community goes far beyond me, and honestly, it's even far beyond them.

> It's a ripple effect: one act of kindness inspiring another, one small gesture of generosity turning into something much bigger than any of us could have imagined.

Remember when we talked about that word *"influencer"*? Well, this is even more proof of just how much impact strangers from the internet can have when they come together for a common purpose. When I first started Wilshire, I thought I was just helping women decorate their homes and get creative. What I didn't realize back then was that God was quietly building something so much deeper: a community that would be the hands and feet of Jesus in action.

Over the years, I've watched this community come together in the most beautiful ways. They've prayed for each other during sickness and loss. They've sent cards, care packages, and words of encouragement to women they've never even met in person. And when real needs have come up, from natural disasters to families facing heartbreak, this community has shown up with open hearts and giving hands. It's humbling and awe-inspiring to watch, because it reminds me that what we've built here isn't about me at all. It's about *us*.

It's about how God can take a group of women connected through crafts and decor and turn them into a force of love and light in a world that can sometimes feel very dark. It starts with something as simple as prayer. I'll never forget being on a Zoom craft night with the DC girls years ago when one of the members shared a struggle she was going through and got emotional.

We stopped right then and there, and we prayed for her. This was the first time I had done this in such a public way within my group. They knew I was a woman of faith, but I had never brought it into the forefront of what I do in that way.

There were tears from both her and me, and many others on that Zoom call. It was so powerful and so touching to see these online friends do that for her. As people continued to post in the DC asking for prayers for various things, I asked them if they'd be interested in a dedicated prayer thread each month so that they could post there to ask for prayers and go there to pray for others.

They, of course, said yes. The amazing thing about this is that since it's a private group, only group members can see it. You don't have to worry about your friend from high school, who you haven't seen in years, knowing your personal business.

These prayers have become a staple of the group and a safe haven. There are many hard and heavy prayer requests every month because life is hard, and we all need prayer. To know that you can post and have hundreds of ladies praying for you is powerful, and it's just the start of the ripple effect.

While not everyone who follows me may be a Christian or share my exact same beliefs, many ladies from the community do turn to me now for those Sunday morning Bible verses that I post and so much more. It's a faith-filled community overall, which is one reason I believe it's so special.

And here's the cool thing: The impact of this faith-filled community reaches farther than we'll ever know. It doesn't stop with all the people inside the Facebook page or the subscriptions. It trickles out into homes, families, and entire communities. That's the kind of impact only God could orchestrate.

I want to share just a couple of the moments that have left me completely speechless. The stories that remind me that this community isn't just something special, but it's something sacred. Before I tell them, I want to reiterate that these stories aren't intended to cast me in a favorable light. This is a God story through and through, and I share these stories entirely for that reason.

———

MELISSA R.'S STORY (TOLD FROM MY PERSPECTIVE)

I would like to tell you the story of Melissa R. and the ripple effect that happened when I met her on that chance day in November.

I was at Target in November of 2022, and I was in a rush, running in for just a few things. There weren't many registers open. So I got in line behind a woman who had a baby in a car seat and a cart that was full of items. I honestly didn't pay too much attention at first until I overheard the cashier asking her how old her baby was. The lady in line told her that he had just turned one and that he was their miracle baby. The cashier could have stopped right there, but she kept asking her questions.

And at this point, I was totally eavesdropping. The mom went on to explain what had happened when her son was born and all the surgeries and trials he had been through since. She had two older kids at home, and she was buying some groceries and some things for them to have little Christmas trees in their rooms, because the prior Christmas they were in the hospital with the baby, and she wanted to make this year special for them.

The cashier asked her if she had any family living nearby to help her. The mom said no, they didn't. This was pulling on every "mom" heartstring I had. I'm surrounded by my family, and all my immediate family lives within a fifteen-mile radius. When I had healthy baby boys, I relied on them so much for help during those younger years. I couldn't imagine doing it alone, let alone with a child with many health struggles and two others at home. My heart was breaking for her in that moment.

As I was fighting back tears, I literally heard God in the Target. (Did you know He goes there? Because He does.) He was telling me to help her, and it was the strongest I've probably ever heard Him speak to me. At that point, I interrupted, and I told her I wanted to pay for her order. She immediately started crying but told me no, she could not let me do that because it was too much, and that some of the stuff she was buying wasn't necessary.

The cashier kept saying to her, "Honey, let her. Let her help you. Let her bless you."

And so she agreed. That mom's name was Melissa, and in that moment, we had an instant connection. We stood in the checkout line of Target crying and hugging each other while a line formed behind us, wondering what was going on. I was so thankful to the cashier, Kelly, for asking the questions so that I could hear part of her story. Not everyone would have done that, and she 100 percent played a huge role in this story.

Melissa didn't know who I was, what I did, or anything about me, of course. I wrote my email address on the back of her receipt, and she wrote her IG handle on the back of mine because she said she wanted to stay in touch.

I was so moved that day in Target and knew I would never forget it. But what I didn't know is that God was not done with our story.

I only told my husband about that story at the time. I immediately told him that I felt such a connection to her, and I hoped that maybe our paths would cross again.

A couple of weeks went by, and I thought about her so much and kept feeling like maybe there was more I could do to help her. I finally decided to reach out to her one day. So I sent her a message on Instagram. She was so happy because she said she had lost her receipt with my info on it and was afraid we would never get connected again. We began forming a friendship over Messenger, and we were making plans to get together soon.

About a month went by, and without planning on it at all, I felt God again telling me to tell the DC group about Melissa and her story. I hesitated on this because I truly believe that when you do good things, you don't need to go around and announce them all the time. There are a lot of people I help, charities I donate to, et cetera, that no one will ever know about.

But for whatever reason, this one felt different. So I was Live in DC one day, and I told them I wanted to share this story about God being at Target. They were all crying through their phone screens, and immediately as I shared what had happened, they said, "How can we help?"

What? I thought. *This community, most of whom do not even know me in person, and none of them know Melissa, wants to help this perfect stranger? They want to collect money for her for Christmas?*

I was overcome with emotion and such pride for this community. So we did it. I asked for her permission to help them and told her how much it meant to my community to be able to do so. She was so appreciative, but I don't think she was expecting what came next.

We raised just over $6,000 for Melissa and her sweet family. I was able to take it to her home along with a goodie basket that we put together for her. And it was the most emotional and powerful moment.

When she opened the check, she was crying and shaking. She had to immediately call her husband to have him confirm what she was telling me. The amount of the check was almost exactly the amount they owed on their son's medical bills, down to the dime.

Hello, Jesus. We see you. Wow.

What an impact… with a ripple effect! It went down from the cashier, Kelly, to me, to Melissa, to my community, and right back around to Melissa and her sweet family. God did that. The trust my community had in me and this story allowed them to open up their hearts to a total stranger whom I met at Target.

I'll never forget it. And I know Melissa and Kelly won't either. Kelly and I hug and chat every time I see her at Target to this day, and Melissa and I still keep in touch.

Full-circle moment in 2023, I invited Melissa to be a guest and surprise the ladies at my live event, many of whom in that room had donated to her just a year prior.

She got to stand on stage with me and tell our story and the story of her sweet son, who's now thriving and doing well. We were able to tell the story of the goodness of God and how this is bigger. Stories like this, whether big or small, have happened so often.

So the next time you feel God speaking to you, even if it's in Target, listen. Lean in. It was so out of my comfort zone to interject in that conversation and offer to do that. I didn't know if she could even use help financially in that way. I didn't know if she would be offended. But God knew. And He wouldn't have laid it on my heart like that if He didn't want me to see it through.

No act of kindness is too big or small. I truly believe that. One small thing can turn someone's day around, and one bigger thing can make an impact on someone's life forever!

Over the years, we have raised money for charities by doing "Give Back" printable bundles and donating a portion to charities like Habitat for Humanity, Samaritan's Purse, and more. I create the printable. The community makes the purchase. We are able to give. And that, my friends, is the ripple effect.

While I wish I could help every single person in need, I know that's not always possible. But we do try to help community members during times of need when we can. This story from Shandra is another great example of that.

———

SHANDRA R.'S STORY

I started following Wilshire Collections in 2018. Stacey's Lives and videos filled my heart with happiness. I enjoyed doing crafts together, and then I joined her decorating community and felt like I had an interior designer at my fingertips to help me decorate my house.

I attended her first live event in 2019 as well. I was finally finishing decorating and putting my house together after years of putting it off. And I was so proud of it.

Then March 3rd, 2020, happened, and our house and town got hit by a tornado. I was devastated because I had just put so much hard work into getting things the way I wanted. I had gotten one of Stacey's decor boxes right before that, and it was one of the things that survived the tornado. It was one of the first things I noticed lying on the floor, and I was so happy to see it there.

It was a little bit of happiness in a very hard time. I had posted in the DC about that box and how happy it made me after the tornado. Stacey reached out to me and felt compelled to do something for me.

I felt so loved in a very hard time. All of our vehicles were totaled, including my husband's work van. One of our first priorities was fixing his truck so he could work, because he's self-employed, so no work equals no paycheck. Stacey began to have the DC raise money to help me out. And she gave me a check that the DC had raised for $1,700.

That very same day, three different families gave us $100. All of it totaled to $2,000, which was the exact amount we needed for the work van. Now that was God loud and clear.

I will never forget it. And I will continue to share that story forever.

And I'll forever be so grateful. God is good all the time.

———

These moments are proof of the ripple effect of the community. I will forever want to pay it forward in any way I can when I can. And while I truly don't believe in announcing every time you do a good deed, I do believe that in times like this, the stories of God's goodness need to be told.

I want you to know that all of this support from my community comes back to trust. Because of the trust I've built with them, they know that when I say, "Hey, send me money for this person in need, or donate to this charity…" that is *exactly* what I'm going to do.

That's why each step in this process of building this business has been so important. Because without their trust in me, these things may not have happened.

Every time I see this community come together, whether it's to pray for someone, to raise money for a family in need, donate to a charity like Habitat for Humanity or St. Jude, or simply encourage a friend who's having a hard day, I'm reminded that what we are building here isn't ordinary. It's extraordinary.

What started with paintbrushes, pillows, and printables has become something beyond my wildest dreams. It's women showing up for one another. It's kindness overflowing into action.

It's proof that God can take the simplest thing, even an online community, and use it to touch hearts, heal wounds, and change lives. The truth is, I may have started Wilshire Collections, but God's the one who breathes life into it. He's the one who turned it into something that's bigger than me, bigger than crafts, and bigger than any plan I could have dreamed up on my own.

It still amazes me how something that started with one simple yes from me, one yes to showing up, to creating, to sharing, has led to thousands of other yeses from women all across the country. Every time one of these ladies chooses to say yes, to help another, to send a card, pray for a stranger, donate to someone in need, it's a reminder that our actions, no matter how small, can carry an eternal impact.

God can take something as simple as a craft project or a Facebook post and use it to spark hope in a heart that needs it the most. These women are everyday wives, moms, grandmas, and friends: women who simply love to create, decorate, and care for others. But that's the beauty of it. God doesn't need perfect people. He uses willing ones. These ladies show up for each other in ways that humble me daily.

This community is full of women who understand that sometimes ministry doesn't happen in a church building. It happens in a Facebook comment, a craft night, or a message that simply says, "Hey, I'm praying for you."

These women don't just pray for each other. They act on it. They give, they show up, and they love deeply. And every time they do, it's a reflection of God's heart moving through this little corner of the internet.

Faith isn't always about grand gestures. Sometimes it looks like a handmade card, a quick donation, or a word of encouragement that arrives at just the right time. That's what this community does so beautifully.

If you are looking for that connection, I know sometimes it can be hard to find, especially the older we get. My advice to you is: find a place where you belong. Find a community that has common interests, morals, and values that you have. Put yourself out there, whether this is in person or online. Because I think the real joy comes from being around like-minded people who have the same interests as you.

At some point, everyone who follows me took the leap and hit that follow button because they saw something they liked along the way. Some of them went on to hit that subscribe button by joining the PC, DC, PCC, or a combo of any of those. They stepped out and probably didn't know what they would get in return.

For some, it's nothing more than decorating and "diy inspo" to them. And that's okay. But to others, the ones who have really leaned in, it's impacting them more than any decorating or DIY tip could.

But the first step is always stepping out and trying something new.

We recently did my Christmas create and decorate week and added a lot of new ladies to the DC and PC. As we do this week together, we get to create and decorate, but I also get to tell them about these groups and how special they are.

The overwhelming response from ladies who joined was, "This is exactly what I've been looking for," or, "I didn't know I was looking for this, but this is going to make me so happy. This is already bringing me so much joy." And that's what it's all about. Taking the leap that just might bring you joy, and opening your heart and mind to let it take you places only God can orchestrate!

Sometimes I step back and think about that scared girl from 2013, painting furniture in her garage during that time. If only she could see this now: not the business, not the numbers, but the impact, the ripple effect. She'd be in awe that God used her love for decorating to bring together a family of women, women who pray, serve, and lift each other up. It's the living, breathing proof that even in the online world, light always wins. When I think about the ripple effect, the joy, the comfort, the hope that's been spread through these women, I'm humbled to my core because I know it's not about me at all. It's about him working through all of us together. And that's the beauty of it.

Every time this community gives, prays, or shows up for someone, the impact spreads far beyond the person on the receiving end.

The woman receiving the blessing feels seen, loved, and cared for, but the women who are giving feel the joy.

It's proof that what we have built here is not just a group, a subscription, or a space for crafting or decorating. It's a ministry. It's a community. It's a connection. It's God using ordinary women to do extraordinary things.

The ripple effect reaches farther than any of us will ever really know. Someone's hope can be restored, someone's faith can be renewed, someone's burden can be lifted, and sometimes their entire life can be changed.

All because a community decided to come together and be the hands and feet of Jesus.

Every single one of you is making a difference. So to every woman who's ever given, prayed, or simply shown up, thank you. You are the heartbeat of this community.

> You're proof that when we walk in faith, love big, and use our gifts to serve others, God multiplies it in ways we could never imagine.

Because at the end of the day, this was never just about crafting or decorating. This is about connection.

This is about community. This is about God. And this will always be bigger.

CHAPTER 9
IMPORTANCE OF LAUGHTER

When I think about the things that haven't changed over all these years, it's who I am at my core. That hot mess express of a girl who loves big, wears her heart on her sleeve, is a people-pleasing, hardworking, God-loving, full of smiles and laughter, family-first kind of girl.

I've always truly loved to laugh. Laughing is at the core of my life and my family's lives. I always say we are a bunch of jokesters, and truly, laughter has gotten us through some of the best and worst times.

Anthony and I like to joke that he's funny because of me, and he says that I'm funny because of him. Maybe we just both bring out the best in each other. Either way, we love to laugh. I'll never forget when we were dating and were out to eat. Anthony purposely put a piece of lettuce in the middle of his two front teeth. When our waitress came up to ask how we were doing, he smiled so big and said, "Doing great!"… lettuce in teeth and all! We cracked up, and there's a very good chance that might have been the moment I knew I was in love.

Anthony's family is *full* of laughter and love, and they love to tell stories as much as I do. He was brought up and raised to laugh and find joy, and I was as well. Having the blend of that from both of our upbringings made it super important for us to have laughter at the core of our marriage and our family.

While our boys' personalities are very different, they are both hilarious in their own ways. There's Parker, with his amazing one-liners, comebacks, and ability to make you belly laugh. And Tyler, from his joke books when he was younger to his now witty and clever personality that can always bring a smile or laugh to your face.

Even though laughter has always been at the core of who I am, when it came to my business, there was a season where I tried so hard to show up polished: hair curled, house spotless, craft prepped, angles right, words rehearsed. And then one day, right in the middle of a Live, I knocked an entire jar of paint over on my table. It went everywhere: my desk, the floor, my shirt... you get the idea.

I froze and just stared at it, thinking, *Should I be mortified and end the Live, or embrace it as my hot-mess self?* Then suddenly, y'all sent out laughing emojis and funny comments, and I started to laugh too. In that moment, I realized something big yet again.

My community didn't want perfect; they wanted real. They wanted the laughter. They wanted the moments that reminded them that we're all just figuring things out. That messy moment broke something open in me in the best way.

As I began to open up over the years on my page and become my true, authentic self, I was able to let more of my humor show. If you've been around my page for more than five minutes, you know something about me. I'm a storyteller, and honestly, I can't *not* be.

I tell stories when I craft, when I decorate, when I shop, when I'm Live, when I'm talking about the boys, when I've had a hot-mess moment, and yes, even when I'm telling on myself. It's just who I am. And over the years, I've learned that storytelling isn't just entertainment; it's connection. When my boys were younger, I would constantly call my mom with funny stories.

This is around the time she started telling me, "You need to be writing this down so you can write a book." I truly wish I had done more of that, because I could have written a good one, but I guess that just wasn't my time. The point is, storytelling is all in how you present it.

Even an ordinary story can be made unforgettable by the way you tell it. I get very expressive in my storytelling, which always makes it more fun. We all have everyday moments, but it's the colors we paint them with, the tone, the energy, the emotion, and the humor that bring them to life.

I've always been a little extra when I tell a story. I use my hands, my face, my voice, my whole personality. I can take a simple trip to TJ Maxx and turn it into a full-blown adventure.

I can describe a crafting fail like it was a scene from a Broadway production. And I'm convinced that half of the fun is the dramatic pause and the "oh my Lanta," the whisper, the giggle, the way I relive it as I retell it. Stories invite people in; they break down walls; they make you feel like you're a friend sitting at the table, not just someone watching through a screen.

I've always believed that an ordinary story becomes extraordinary when you tell it with honesty, humor, and heart. And that's exactly what I try to do every single time I show up. Sometimes I'm animated and dramatic. Sometimes I'm laughing so hard that I snort. It happens, y'all. And sometimes I'm sharing something tender that brings tears instead, but it all matters because stories are where we find ourselves.

They're where we realize we're not alone. And oh my Lanta, laughter is its own kind of ministry, isn't it? If crafting has taught me anything, it's that you have to be willing to laugh at yourself. Hot glue fails, crooked bows, printable bubbles, paint spills, losing my scissors eighty-four times a day, whisper-shopping when people are staring at me. It's all comedy gold. And the best part is we laugh together. That's the magic.

But here's the beautiful thing: when you tell a story with heart, whether it's silly, playful, painful, embarrassing, or ordinary, people lean in. They see themselves in it. They laugh with you, cry with you, and connect with you in a deeper way than you even realize. That's the magic of storytelling.

It turns little moments into shared moments, and it takes everyday life and turns it into something memorable. And honestly, that's one of the reasons this community is what it is today.

> Because when you let people into your stories, the real ones, the funny ones, the messy ones, it builds connection, it builds trust, and it reminds us that we're all a little more alike than we think.

Storytelling isn't about perfection. It's about presence. It's about emotion. It's about saying, "Here's my life, the good, the bad, the ridiculous, and you're welcome to come along for the ride." And that's what I hope people continue to feel here: like we're sitting on the couch together, laughing until we cry over the most ordinary moments, just because the story brought us there. It doesn't hurt that somehow adventures always seem to follow me.

And I love bringing my community along on those crazy adventures and telling them about the funny times. Maybe some of these are your favorites that you've heard me tell over the years. Like when I tried to walk across the SkyBridge in Gatlinburg with shaky legs as my family ran ahead of me to get over it fast, while I stood there, paralyzed in fear, feeling like each of my legs weighed 999 pounds.

Or like the time we did a snorkeling adventure on a vacation, and the boat dropped us off in the middle of the ocean and made us swim what felt like ten miles to shore to enjoy all of ten minutes on a beach. I called it my first triathlon because we walked miles to get there, swam miles, and then I sat on a noodle to paddle my way back to the boat, which became my bike. (Go ahead and give me my medal now.)

Or the time I chased my receipt through a parking lot, and it landed right in front of the door to Marshall's, which of course was God telling me, "Go shop, girl." Or the time my family convinced me to go snow tubing, but it turns out it was ice, and it turns out I didn't quite make it down in one piece. Funny how we can laugh about that one now.

Maybe it was the time my dress was tucked in my underwear in public, not once, but twice. Oh, wait, maybe it was the time I found a cicada in my shirt and lost my mind, or the time I almost swallowed a bee. You get the idea.

If it's funny, more than likely they're gonna be hearing the story. But then sometimes those funny things, well, they aren't retold on a Live because they happen *on* a Live. One thing I've learned after years of going Live is this: you cannot escape the funny moments, so you might as well embrace them.

And honestly, those are usually the moments that the community loves the most. Something unexpected will happen. I'll lose my scissors for the forty-seventh time. I'll have a hot glue emergency. I'll say the wrong word, drop something, or completely botch whatever I'm trying to do. And instead of pretending it didn't happen, I just roll with it.

Because here's the truth: life is messy, crafting is messy, and Live videos are very messy. And that's exactly what makes them real. I've had moments where I'm laughing so hard I can't breathe. Those moments remind every woman watching that she doesn't have to be perfect either. Perfection is boring, but authenticity… It's relatable.

And laughter, that's a universal connector. So now when something goes sideways in life, I don't panic. I just smile, laugh, and bring everyone along for the chaos because that's life, that's crafting, that's community, and that's where the best memories get made.

I used to think I needed to show up perfect. Now I know that the imperfect moments are the ones people relate to the most. When I laugh at myself, it gives other women permission to do the same, to stop being so hard on themselves and just enjoy being human. Some of my closest bonds with the community came from the moments where we were crying laughing over something that wasn't planned. Those moments weren't part of a business strategy. They were as "real life" as you could get.

And boy, do I have some favorites. We can't forget the infamous Spidergate of 2021, probably the one I'm most well-known for. It was the moment when I was Live wearing an elf hat, no less, for a Christmas workshop, and I was crafting but couldn't find my bow. Suddenly, I felt something on my toe and thought, *Could that be the bow that I feel on my toe?*

It was in that moment that I looked down and realized that it was a spider! I screamed like I've never screamed before and yelled for Anthony, and he came running as I was in the corner screaming, "Get it, get it!" No one watching knew what I was screaming about. Some thought it was a mouse, maybe a snake, but nope, a spider. Anthony came in to save the day and scooped it up in a paper towel to put it outside.

I told him to first show everybody how big it was, but not to let it crawl. The moment he opened the paper towel and showed it to my viewers, it jumped out of the paper towel and onto my table. I started screaming again, and my boys came running down to see what was wrong.

Once my fear subsided and the spider was gone, we were instantly all able to laugh about what had happened. It's things like this that are real life and real moments beyond our control, but it's also something people still talk about to this day.

Then there was the time I was Live and you could see my front side-walk from the craft room window. I saw a sales guy head up to the door, and we almost made eye contact. I immediately ducked and hid under my desk, all while whispering, "Shh, I'll be back. I'm hiding from someone." They got the biggest kick out of that because who hasn't done that at some point? If I don't know you, I am not coming to the door. Sorry, not sorry.

What about the time I somehow accidentally went Live from my pocket while cleaning out the garage with Anthony? If you know how projects like that go with married couples, I was mortified when my friend Vanessa called me to tell me I was Live because I was thinking, *Oh no, what did we say?* The Live was around three minutes long, and when we watched it back, oh my goodness, the laughs it caused. Luckily, we didn't say anything bad, so I ended up leaving it for people to continue to watch, and it was hysterical: me asking Alexa how to convert centimeters to feet for a rug size, and then me also asking Anthony what we should do with an old blanket I found with mouse poop on it, and him yelling, "We're keeping it!" It was a true behind-the-scenes, real-life moment for all to witness. However, I am extra careful and paranoid now about those accidental Lives.

Then there was the time I went Live from the top of a Colorado mountain when I got separated from my family and was alone, cold, and afraid to ski down by myself. The way you guys talked me down that mountain is something I'll never forget.

You had to laugh, or else you would have cried. (Okay, maybe I did cry a little.) There are so many other funny moments and mishaps from Lives that I couldn't begin to share them all.

I've spilled paint and Mod Podge and even stain, messed up projects, burned myself with a glue gun, and so much more. And you know what? All of those things help show people that everyone makes mistakes, even us professionals. I love what Barbara R. wrote, and I hope that many feel the same way about the laughter and smiles that just might come your way when you're a part of this community.

———

BARBARA R.'S STORY

There's something about her laughter, genuine, effortless, and full of light, that always has a way of turning my day around.

It's more than just a sound. It's like a ripple of happiness that spreads through everything she touches. She has this incredible gift of making everything seem fun and easy.

Even on my worst day, she finds a way to make me laugh, even when I don't feel like laughing. Her humor is a light in any room, and it's no surprise that it's woven into everything she does.

Her craft: it's not just about printables or creating adorable pillows, though she's a genius at both. It's about building a space, a community where everyone feels like they belong. Each printable she designs and each pillow she creates isn't just a project but an invitation. She invites you to join her world, to laugh with her, and to become part of something bigger.

A group of crafters who are bound together by more than just paper and fabric. We're bound by the joy she brings. Her laughter isn't just a sound; it's a thread that runs through everything she creates.

When she asked about contributing to her new book, I knew immediately what I wanted to say. The best thing she always does is make me laugh. It's the kind of laughter that makes everything seem possible, that brings us together as a community of crafters, no matter where we are.

———

Just like laughter is important to me within my family and business, it's important to me in friendships too. I love to go deep and have meaningful friendships, but I also love when you can be with someone and just belly laugh over the silliest things.

I'm pretty lucky to have some hilarious friends who share this love of laughter with me! One person who always comes to mind is Kristy from Kristy's Craft Room. Wherever we go and whatever we do, we are usually cutting up and laughing as we do it. Because Kristy and I share such a similar love and zest for life, it's easy for us to work together and collaborate.

The first time we met in person, Kristy accidentally whacked me in the head with her coffee cup. We both cracked up, and I knew in that moment we were going to get along great! We both have amazing communities who trust us, come to us for drama-free fun, and lean on us for crafting ideas and inspiration.

Being able to partner with Kristy on collaborations like the Simple Swap Frames and my upcoming 2026 live event has been nothing short of a blast. She's someone I trust 100 percent with anything I do. And when you can combine friendship with business and laughter… that's the perfect combo!

But do you wanna know a secret?

There have been plenty of days that I've had to show up Live when laughing, or even smiling, felt like the farthest thing from my mind. But every time that happens, I somehow manage to smile and laugh.

Laughter doesn't mean you ignore the hard things. It just keeps the hard things from stealing the show. And I know the only reason I'm able to do this is that I genuinely love what I do, and it does bring me happiness, even on my hardest days. There's something powerful that happens when women laugh together.

Walls come down, worries take a backseat, and your heart feels lighter. Laughter creates instant connection, the kind that makes even strangers feel like old friends having a girls' night together. I didn't always realize the impact joy had, but I've learned something important over the years.

Joy is part of this ministry. God didn't just give me a creative gift. He gave me the gift of storytelling and the gift of spreading laughter. So you better believe I'm going to put those gifts to good use and spread joy whenever I can.

I've learned that laughter doesn't mean life is perfect. It means you're choosing joy in the middle of mess and chaos. And sometimes that joy is exactly what someone else needs to breathe a little easier that day.

As I look back on all the stories, the belly laughs, the whisper-shopping mishaps, the hot glue disasters, and the moments where everything went sideways on a Live, I realized something so simple but so true:

Joy is contagious, laughter is healing, and real moments are what bind us together.

This chapter isn't just about being funny or telling stories. It's about letting yourself be human. It's about showing up exactly as you are, even when the bow is crooked, the printable bun bubbles, or the spiders crawl on your toe.

It's about letting people see you, the real you, the imperfect you, the you who laughs at herself and keeps going anyway. And here's the thing: these moments, the unplanned ones, the silly ones, the ones that are really just happy ones, are often the ones God uses the most because they remind us not to take life too seriously. They remind us we're not alone, and they remind us that connection grows where perfection ends.

If this community has taught me anything, it's that joy can live right in the middle of a mess. And when we choose to share that joy through stories, laughter, vulnerability, and real-life moments, we create something bigger than a craft, bigger than a pretty home; we create belonging.

So as you turn the page and move into the next part of this book, I hope you carry this with you: Don't be afraid to tell your story. Don't be afraid to laugh at the messy parts. And don't be afraid to let others in, even when things aren't perfect. Because somewhere out there, someone needs the exact joy you bring.

And often, it's the imperfect moments that shine the brightest. If there's one thing I hope people take from the time they spend with me, it's that they know laughter is allowed here. Joy is welcome here.

And no matter how hard life gets, we don't have to walk through it alone. We can laugh our way through the messy parts together. I want to always keep laughter at the center of my life.

There are plenty of times and moments in life when you need to be serious. Save your energy for those big moments and those hard moments that require you to be serious.

And in the not-so-serious moments, let your guard down. Laughter is the best medicine, and there's truly nothing better than a good ol' belly laugh!

People may originally come for the decorating ideas or the cute crafts, but my hope is that they stay for the stories, for the belly laughs, for the joy. That is the exact impact I hope I can leave on this community to let people know that this is bigger.

CHAPTER 10
FAMILY, BALANCE, AND BEING PRESENT

F amily is literally my everything, and man, do I have a good one. I have said so many times that I wouldn't still be doing what I'm doing today without the unwavering support from Anthony.

From day one, he hauled furniture, cheered me on, and helped me navigate starting this business. He's now at every event I host. He listens when I'm excited or upset.

He helps me when needed, goes Live with me from time to time, and makes funny reels with me when I ask him, and let's not forget that he cooks, too. He's my best friend and soulmate and the most incredible dad. And if he hadn't been cheering me on during all of those hard years, and even the good ones too, I would have quit long ago.

I'm not sure he will ever realize how crucial he is to Wilshire and its success. And let me just say, the ladies from the community love him, too. From his attempted skipping video and being my spider rescue hero to popping online to craft with me, cooking from the kitchen, or meeting those at a live event, our community has embraced him, and he loves them right back. He knows many names from the community. He's met some of them in person, and he's truly invested in every aspect of my business. He knows the names of many, faces of a lot, and is truly invested in all of it. Sometimes those behind-the-scenes support roles are just as important as anything forward-facing.

One cute, sweet, and cheesy thing that Anthony does when I'm having a bad day is tell me exactly what he knows will make me smile each time. You see, I may need to mention that "words of affirmation" is my love language, so a few positive sentences go a long way with me. When he knows I've had a bad day, he will give me a big hug and say, "You're good enough, you're smart enough, and gosh darn it, people love you."

Which is a quote from an old *Saturday Night Live* skit. Every time he says it, I smile, and every time it makes me feel better because he's telling me that I'm enough, that what I'm doing matters, to keep going, to not give up, and that he's proud. He doesn't need to say anything else for me to know that all of those things are true.

For those who have had the honor of hearing him speak at my live events, you know how sincere and heartfelt he is and how he truly feels about me and this community. He wanted to include a little something for the book, so here it is.

―――――

A NOTE FROM ANTHONY

Stacey, I want to first off say how proud I am of you.

To witness what you've created is nothing short of amazing. I've been here since day one and have been through all of the ups, the downs, and all of the pivots in between. You work hard, and your dedication shows in everything that you do.

What is so special is that I see the love you have for your community that you've created. I see the behind-the-scenes and the effort you put in daily to make sure the community has a fun experience. It truly shows in all that you have created.

I'm not shocked about the love you have from so many strangers because you are impossible not to love. You are real, and everyone can see it. You have blessed so many with your words, wisdom, and humor.

Not only have you helped people with their decor, but you have helped many through tough times in their own lives just by popping on a Live and allowing them to laugh, craft, and just take a breath. God has blessed you with a gift of compassion, hard work, creativity, and dedication, and it's a pleasure to be a small part of it. You've shown our boys that dreams are possible if you work hard enough to achieve them.

Congratulations on finally getting to fulfill another dream of yours by writing this book. It will be amazing, and I cannot wait to see the finished result. I love you, Anthony.

———

All these years later, his words and love for me still give me goosebumps, and man, do I love him right back.

Anthony, I'll never be able to thank you enough for your unconditional love and support, not only in life but in business as well. You've excelled in your own career, all while allowing me to chase my dreams right next to you.

You're a hard worker, a dedicated husband, and the best dad to our boys. You always have the right words to make me smile or laugh, and I love how we balance each other out, with your laid-back, go-with-the-flow personality and mine, which is, well, the opposite. I love you so much, and after all these years, we still go together like peanut butter and jelly... but better.

And then we have my sweet boys, Parker (19) and Tyler (14). They have literally grown up watching their mom have this online business. From being in the garage helping me paint back in 2013 to everything in between, they've seen it all.

I will never forget how real it all became for them at my first live event in 2019, just like it did for me. For them to get to meet these ladies was incredible. The ladies brought them gifts, and everyone even signed Tyler's joke book for him. How incredible!

It's now normal for them to be with me when I get recognized in public, and they even get recognized, too. They come to all of my events, help with set up and tear down, and talk with everyone there.

I remember Parker asking me if I was going to have security at my 2023 event, to which I said, "Why do you think I need security?" He was worried that someone was going to come who shouldn't have been there and go a little crazy, so we joked that we were going to get him a security shirt and put him by the door as people came in. The fact that he felt a level of protectiveness for me meant the world to me.

When they were younger, they were all about being on camera with me, especially my youngest, Tyler, who often went Live crafting with me. Tyler coming on Live and telling his jokes is something I will never forget.

Those were such special times and some true core memories. There was a time when Tyler was Live with me, and someone left a really rude comment about him. My mama bear came out, and hundreds of other mama bear claws came out, too. I sent him out of the room to protect his little heart as I addressed what was said. At that moment, I realized Tyler had hundreds of mama bears supporting him. I don't think they will ever know what that day meant to me and how they helped me through it.

It was also a bit of an eye-opening moment for me, realizing the negative side to putting my kids out there on the internet in that way. I would be lying if I didn't tell you that it caused a little guard to go up.

Something I've tried really hard to do over the years is respect their boundaries. It's hard putting your life out on the internet and finding the balance between wanting to share and having some privacy. The older they each got, the more privacy they wanted, and I understand 100 percent and respect that.

My oldest, Parker, has always been so supportive but is definitely the more private of the two. I would be lying if I said that at first it didn't bother me a little. I would joke with him that the community needed "proof of life" to know he was still around and part of the family. But the more I listened to his wishes, the more I understood.

It's strange to be at school and have a teacher come up to you and say, "Oh, I saw you went to the movies yesterday. Did you have fun?" all because they saw it on his mom's public Facebook page.

I won't post pictures of them without their permission now. I don't share personal things without them knowing, and I would never make them do something they didn't want to do. It's a fine line, and one I feel is personal to each family that's in a public role like this.

And as much as I sometimes want to post every little thing they do, tell every cute and funny story, etc., I don't, because their wishes mean more to me than any of that. And I have Parker to thank for opening my eyes to that. And to be honest, I like having stuff for just us. I like feeling like not everything we do as a family has to be shared on social media. Moments for just us. Memories for just us, without the Wilshire.

We've had so many ups and downs in our behind-the-scenes family life that will never be shared publicly. We've gone through some real challenges and faced hard parenting decisions, as most parents do.

We've had victories and celebrations and just all the normal things family life brings. Inside my Decorating and Creating Community, I'm able to open up and share more about my family because it's a safe space inside a private group with no trolls, no haters, and no negativity, only 100 percent love and support. They were there for me as we faced some really hard parenting decisions with support, advice, and zero judgment.

As far as the public goes, I now share only as much as they are comfortable with. And when I do, the community is there and always asking about them. They were there to support me as we navigated sending Parker off to college for the first time (cue all the feels).

They were there with Tyler and his LTS shirts (story to come below) and now ask about how his basketball is going. They are invested in me, in my family, in our happiness. And wow, how incredible it is to have so many people who care about you.

You aren't getting to see all there is to my boys. And I know if you knew them more, you would love them just like we do. They are looking more alike the older they get, but their personalities couldn't be more different. But they are both amazing in their own ways, and you'll have to trust me on that!

But here are a few things you need to know. They love their mama and their dad, too. And they both love family time, our dinners out, our travels, our pool time, our traditions… and they are proud.

They help me move and haul, get seasonal bins down, go to my events, and more. They ask if I have any videos going viral, and they don't like it when I get hate comments or messages. They often try to tell me exactly what I should draft in response to those people, a.k.a., they're protective.

They know all about the DC girls, PC girls, and Pillow Besties and ask about them often. They see the hard work Anthony and I both put into our careers, and they also see the rewards from that hard work.

And I hope they don't take any of that for granted. I hope they know that so much of what we do is for them and their futures.

To my boys, thank you for embracing this crazy job of mine.

Thank you for being by my side when you were little and staying with me as you continued to grow.

Thank you for being honest with me about your boundaries and helping me realize how important those are.

Thank you for your hilarious sense of humor.

And thank you for giving me the honor of being your mom. It's one of my greatest gifts in life, and I love you both so much.

Something I hope none of us ever forget is the story of Literally Too Soft…

When my son Tyler was eight years old, he came to us and told us he wanted to sell T-shirts that were super soft and raise money for sick kids in hospitals. He said he wanted to call the shirts Literally Too Soft, or "LTS" for short. We, of course, thought it was adorable but didn't think too much about it at first. He kept talking about it, even coming up with his own little kid business plan.

So one Christmas, we decided to get him a shirt made, a soft shirt with "Literally Too Soft" printed on it. His little wish came true, and out of all the presents he got that Christmas, that was his favorite. From there, we told the community about this, and once they heard about it, they were all in on supporting his dream.

We got to work, designed a logo together, and started having shirts made that were (you guessed it) literally too soft. He was very set on helping sick kids in hospitals, and after talking to him about it, we made the decision to donate a portion of the proceeds to St. Jude's. We did several releases over the course of a few years, sold hundreds and hundreds of shirts, and were able to donate thousands of dollars to St. Jude to help sick kids in hospitals. Ladies bought these soft LTS shirts for themselves, their kids, grandkids, and even their husbands. We worked out the payment for Tyler for his help in packing them up and getting them shipped out, which could go into his savings. Tyler didn't want Parker to be left out, so he decided to give him a cut of his payment if he would help us pack.

So as a family, we would stand around our dining room table, shirts piled high, and pack those orders. This was Tyler's dream, but it was a family mission, and one that you all made possible. I will never forget those days, and I know my family won't either.

To this day, when I see someone wearing one, my heart bursts with absolute pride. Tyler has that little entrepreneurial spirit in him, with a heart of gold mixed in. I will forever think of that time with such fond memories.

To make a little boy's dream come true like that was truly special. LTS is on pause right now, but you never know when, or if, it might make its return one day. My little family of four is, of course, my world, but it's been really cool to also let the community in to get to know more of my extended family as well.

You'll find my dad often popping on my Facebook Lives, and I always joke and tell people, "It's okay, y'all, that's my dad, not some troll," because let's face it, I don't get many men watching my videos. My mom is always scrolling through the comments and telling me what she read or how sweet all of you are. She also loves it when I share pictures or videos of *her* beautiful decorating at her home or the lake house, and the ladies love seeing it all too!

I have done fashion videos with my sister, which is way out of my comfort zone, but she made it easy, and y'all love it when we do content together. It's something I hope we can continue to do more of. She's at all of my live events and is a phone call (or quick drive) away when I need to talk!

Anthony's family has always loved me like I am their own. They follow along, they support me, and they stand up for me when they see me being attacked in the comments. They are so protective of me, and I love them so much for that. They also raised an incredible son, whom I will be forever grateful for.

Many of you have been able to meet my sweet family members at my live events, and you ask about them often, which is just truly so sweet.

Bottom line: what I do is a family affair, and without their love and support, I just don't know how I could do it, to be honest.

One thing that's super important to my family and me is travel. I was blessed to be able to travel when I was a child, and I hold those memories close.

Anthony and I have been intentional about making travel a priority in our lives. I would always rather give and get an experience any day over a gift. My boys are the same way and have grown to love it as much as we do.

We've taken some amazing trips, and some of our funniest family moments come from those trips.

As the boys get older, I realize even more just how much those trips mean, and just how valuable that family time is. With one out of the house and one with a busier social and sports life than Anthony and I combined, it's harder and harder to find those moments together, but it makes me cherish them so much more when they happen. I hope they carry this love of travel over into their families one day, because I truly think it's so important.

Thank you for loving my family and being so invested. You may not know or see it all, but you are there, and I know that. You're supportive, caring, and in our corner, and I love you for it.

Here's the thing about family, though, and where the truth bomb gets dropped. Are we close? Yes. Do we love to spend time together? Also yes. Is it always perfect? Nope. No family is, of course. We've had our fair share of bad and hard days.

That's life, and that's family. For a long time, I struggled with this quiet little guilt tucked away in the back of my mind, the guilt of wanting more for my life, more for my business, more for my creativity, more ways to grow, impact, and dream. Maybe you've felt it too, that tug of war between loving your family with your whole heart but also feeling this spark inside you that whispers, "There's something more here."

You were made for this, too. For years, I thought wanting more meant I was somehow being selfish. Like if I reached for something beyond motherhood, it meant I wasn't grateful for what I already had.

But here's what I've learned.

> Wanting more for your life doesn't mean you love your family any less. It means you're honoring the gifts God placed inside you.

God doesn't give us passions, talents, and dreams just to let them sit quietly in a corner. He gives them to us because He intends for us to use them, to serve, to create, to inspire, to bring joy, and to impact others in ways only we can. And wanting more doesn't mean you're chasing success. It means you're chasing purpose. It means you're growing. It means you're listening. It means you're stepping into your calling, even when it feels scary or uncertain.

And here's something I want every woman reading this to hear loud and clear: You can love your family deeply and still want more for yourself. You can chase your dreams and raise babies with your whole heart. You can pursue creativity, build a business, make an impact, and still be an amazing mom, wife, and friend. Your desire for more is not something to hide or apologize for.

It's something to honor, and it's something to celebrate. Because when women step into their gifts, everybody around them rises, too. I truly believe my boys are watching me not just build a business, but build resilience, courage, creativity, faith, and purpose. And I hope one day they look back and say, "Mom didn't just tell us to chase dreams. She showed us how."

So if you've ever felt guilty for wanting more, please let that go. You're not being selfish; you're being obedient. You're walking in what God placed inside you for a reason. And the world, your world, is better because you did.

And here's the beautiful part. Even as I learned to give myself permission to want more and to dream big, to grow this business God placed in my heart, I also had to learn something just as important: more doesn't mean at the expense of the people you love most. Chasing my calling didn't erase my role as a wife and mom; it made me even more aware of how much I wanted to nurture both.

The more my business grew, the more intentional I had to become about making space for my family, faith, rest, and real-life moments off-screen. Wanting more for your life and building something meaningful can coexist with being present with your family, but only if you learn how to balance the two.

And let me just tell you, balance didn't come naturally. It was something I had to learn, unlearn, and learn again, and something I'm still learning.

It took boundaries, choices, sacrifice, grace, and sometimes a whole lot of trial and error. I found myself asking, *How do I grow the dream God gave me without missing the moments God gave me that are right in front of me?* The question became the heart of my next lesson, one that shaped not just my business, but my home, my peace, and my purpose. Let's talk about it: the messy, honest, beautiful dance of family and balance.

I have to admit, there was a season of building Wilshire where my work–life balance was, well, pretty much non-existent. I'm talking late nights, early mornings, weekends filled with projects, holidays spent answering messages, and more screen time than I'd ever want to confess to. I was hustling so hard that I barely had time to breathe, much less rest, take care of myself, or be fully present 24/7 with my family. And you know what? I carried guilt over that for a long time. But at the end of the day, I don't regret those years because they were necessary at that stage of my business. They built the foundation. They created the community we have today.

But looking back, I can also admit that I missed some things, and that stings a little. There were nights I tucked my boys in and then picked my phone right back up. There were Saturdays when I should have been at the park with my family, but instead I was answering customer emails. There were times Anthony wanted to watch a movie with me, and I was still editing photos or prepping a craft. He never complained, bless him, but I felt the pull.

Some of you may remember when I had Wilshire Place, which was a little townhouse I rented for all things Wilshire. I set up an office, a craft space, and a shipping hub there. The truth is, I was struggling with balance at the time I got the townhouse, and I thought that having work removed from my home would help with that. That way, when I closed the townhouse doors in the afternoon, I could drive home and be done with work.

And guess what? It worked. It was during that time that I was finally able to create a little separation between the two, and it taught me so many valuable lessons.

Once we built our new house and I had better dedicated spaces to craft in, work in, etc., I decided to give the townhouse up. And I haven't looked back.

I'm proud to say I've carried over what I learned from those Wilshire Place years into the now. I know when to shut the office or craft room doors. I take (most) Fridays off and make that a priority. In the summer, I work an even more modified schedule so that I can spend time with my family and float in my pool. I'm making my business work for me and my schedule, and not letting the business run my life.

Because the truth is, I don't want my kids or my husband to remember me as the mom and wife who was always on her phone. I want them to remember me as the mom who worked hard, yes, but who also knew when to put the phone down, close the laptop, and choose quality time. I want them to remember the cuddles, the laughs, the dinners around the table, the vacations, the movie nights, the cheering from the sidelines, and not the constant glow of a screen.

So over the years, I've worked really hard to create boundaries: to shut the office door at a certain time, to put my phone away when we're eating dinner, to take days off, to be intentional with my yes's and protective of my no's. It hasn't been perfect because I'm not perfect, but oh my Lanta, I've gotten better, and it has been worth it. Now, work doesn't control my life.

I love my business, but I love my family more. I always have, but in the beginning and before I had the help of a team, there simply wasn't enough of me to go around, and I felt pulled so many times. I've learned that the world won't fall apart if I don't respond to a message immediately, that life will go on if there's a week I can't show up Live, and that it's okay to take a full week off and go on vacation with my family. I can slow down, be present, and still keep building and running my business.

These changes didn't happen overnight, and as I said, I still work on them daily. It took honest conversations within my household to get me on the right track, and it requires being intentional and setting boundaries. It requires saying no sometimes. It requires persistence.

People ask me a lot why I don't go Live more at night. I know that might be a more convenient time for some who work during the day, but the bottom line is that daytime is when I work. My nights are for my family and me, and I don't need to apologize for that.

When time and space allow, I'll throw in an evening Live, but I try very hard to have normal working hours like anyone else in most nine-to-five jobs. What has surprised me the most is that the more present I became at home, the more peace I found in my business. My creativity grew, my joy grew, my energy grew, and my calling became clearer, because a rested, present version of me is always better than the over-worked, stretched-thin, burned-out version.

I hope this encourages someone reading, whether you're running a business, managing a household, or doing both, that it's okay to pause, it's okay to rest, and it's okay to let work be work and let your family be your heart. Because at the end of the day, your family doesn't want perfect; they just want you. I'm not perfect in this area, and I'm not sure 100 percent balance is ever going to be possible, but it's something I will keep striving for every day.

What my family has taught me is that multiple things can coexist. You can be a great mom, wife, daughter, friend, and business owner all at once. Some days the business might take more of your energy, some days it's your kids, then the next, your husband, and then a friend or family member in need. The important thing is that you show up for people and things in your life when they are needed the most.

But I've also learned that showing up doesn't always look the same in every season. Sometimes it's being fully present at home, sometimes it's focusing on work because God is opening a door, sometimes it's being still, resting, and letting yourself breathe, and sometimes it's giving what little you have left, even if it's just a smile, a hug, or a whispered prayer.

> Balance isn't about doing everything perfectly; it's about knowing what matters most right now and giving your heart to that.

Because I've learned that being everything to everyone is impossible, but being present where it matters is doable, and that's the real win.

But let's be honest, you can't show up for anyone if you're running on empty. Balance sometimes means saying no. It means taking a break. It means letting the laundry wait so you can watch a movie with your kid or stepping away from your phone so you can breathe again. I'm not always the best at taking time for myself, and I know many other women struggle with this too, but it's something I'm actively working on.

A little over a year ago, I made the decision to do a once-a-quarter spa day, where I would go away for a whole day to get pampered. I've stuck to it and enjoyed it so much. I love to binge-watch a show, lie in my bed and scroll TikTok, take long baths, go shopping just for me without recording content, and spend time with friends. And of course, float in my pool and spend time at the lake when I can, which has become my favorite outlet of all. All of these things fill my cup, and that is what we need as women. So give yourself grace and permission to rest. Allow yourself to go all in on your passions and not feel guilty for having the desire to work hard, but allow yourself to be present for your family in the moments that matter the most.

What I know for sure is this: balance is a work in progress, and I'm a work in progress too, but somehow even in the chaos, God weaves it all together: my family, my business, and my calling. When I show up for what matters most, everything else falls into place exactly as it should.

And that, my friends, is the real beauty of balance. God brings it all together in a way that reminds me that this whole journey is much bigger than I ever dreamed.

CHAPTER 11
FINDING PURPOSE
IN THE PIVOTS

The year 2023 marked ten years in business. And as you can tell, my business has looked a lot of different ways over those years. My boys went from "littles" to teens, and my husband was by my side through all the ups and downs. If you had told "2013 Stacey" what "2023 Stacey" was going to be up to, she would not have believed you.

In 2023, I had a rare opportunity to go back to my childhood home before they tore it down. When I entered my old childhood bedroom, the one I had once sponge-painted the walls in hot pink, I rounded the corner to see pink walls and a chalkboard wall where some little girl had written, *"Nevertheless, she persisted."* I nearly broke down in tears. A little girl lived in that same house, in that same room, as I once did. And something was in her that may have been in me all along, too: strength to know that no matter what life throws at you, you have to keep going. This has since become such a mantra for me.

And it has shown up in my life time and time again, as you are about to see in this chapter. Things were holding steady for a couple of years, and I spent time curating an even better experience for the community by adding in things like throw blankets, lumbar pillows, and more to the product lineup to coordinate with their pillows, printables, etc. We began going on what I call "journeys of cuteness and coordination," and man, have they been cute.

Life was good. It was really good, in fact. And I was counting each blessing and living out my dream that I had worked so hard to build. I hit a huge milestone in my business at the end of 2024 and was just over the moon going into the new year. All the years of hard work and dedication were paying off tenfold, and I couldn't wait to see what was next. I had no clue just how hard that next year was going to be.

One thing I still struggled with was balance, as I mentioned in the previous chapter. Being able to focus on what's important in that moment didn't come naturally to me, and I was feeling like I was being pulled in a million different directions at any given moment. So when 2025 started, I picked *"balance"* as my word of the year. But it quickly became apparent that my real word was *pivot*.

In 2025, I experienced blows that I didn't see coming in my life, my family's, friends', and my team's. Everything from health scares and setbacks, surgeries and injuries, and diagnoses to feeling the weight of the world and the economy shift in my business. Oh, and sending our oldest off to college. I won't be going into any of these things in great detail because so many of these things are not my story to tell. But here's what I can tell you: when things like this are going on behind the scenes, it makes doubt creep in.

It makes you question it all at times. It makes it harder to show up as your true self, and it makes you even more appreciative of the times when all is going smoothly. It's especially hard when there are things going on with family or friends that I'm just not at liberty to speak about publicly.

But on the inside, my heart is heavy. I'm worried, I'm anxious, and I'm stressed. At times, I was able to share the pivots that came along, and many of you know that "pivot" became a word around here this year.

I had put off a surgery longer than I should have and finally had it all set for January 2025. I'm such a planner, so I picked the *perfect* time to finally have this surgery, at a slower time of the year, when I could block the calendar off and not be stressed about taking time to recover. I got the whole plan in place with my team on how they would help me during that time. We were organized and ready.

And then, the first pivot happened.

The night before my surgery, I got extremely sick, so you guessed it: surgery canceled! I never thought I would say I'd be sad to not have surgery, but I was so bummed. I was instantly stressed about when it would get rescheduled and how we would pivot and adjust the calendar, plans, etc. Was this the end of the world? Of course not. But it felt big to me in that moment.

And it also taught me a lesson. I can be the biggest planner out there, but things don't always go according to our plans; they go according to His. I had to tell myself that maybe He was protecting me from something I'll never know about on that original surgery day. Again, I had to trust.

The surgery got rescheduled for the middle of February, and once I had a date, my team and I began to pivot, move things around, and figure it out.

One thing about me is that *I do not like to reschedule things*, be late, etc. So if I say I'm going to be Live in DC on this day at this time, I'm going to be there unless something big happens where I truly just can't.

Did I have to cancel things, back out of commitments, and more? Sure did.

Did the show go on? Yep.

Did everyone understand? Of course they did!

The surgery I had turned out to be a significant life lesson for me and my planning mentality.

This situation reminded me that sometimes, life forces you to slow down. It was as if God was telling me to take a breath and realize that life would continue and everything would be okay. I learned that schedules can be adjusted, and nobody was upset or angry about the change. In fact, people expressed their sympathy and wanted to support me in any way they could.

In the moment, I thought rescheduling the surgery was the end of the world. However, it ended up teaching me a valuable lesson along the way. Little did I know, this would be the first of many pivots this year and that my extra faith and extra trust were just starting to get ramped up!

Right before my rescheduled surgery, Kellie, who works for me, ended up having emergency surgery and being in the hospital for weeks. It was a very scary time for her and all who love her. She was sad she couldn't be there for me, and I was sad I couldn't be there for her. We would text and FaceTime and just cry together over all that was going on. We prayed, and we prayed big.

I went into my surgery and came home to recover, all while she was still in the hospital. Eventually, she recovered and went home, and we had the best reunion, poolside in our PJs. It felt like we had been through so much already in just the first few months of the year!

The way this community rallied and prayed for both of us during that time is something neither of us will ever forget. Work things had to be put on hold, things had to be rescheduled, and every one of you gave us both grace. You gave us time to rest, recover, and get back on our feet.

Just a couple of months later, we were set to host Wilshire Live 2025, which felt like a big undertaking when all of that happened, and we were out of commission. But we did it and pulled off an *amazing* event thanks to many others who helped us!

All of that to say, my online community knows a lot about my life… but there are some things they haven't known, especially from 2025, that I want to keep private. Still, I think it's important for you all to know some of the real and the raw so you don't read this book and think that it's all been easy, because it's been far from that. I, too, am human and have real-life problems I face every single day, and I'm sure you realize that.

Life hasn't been perfect; this past year has been hard, messy, and full of ups and downs and twists and turns. At times, if I'm honest, it felt like the blows just kept coming.

I prayed for balance, but God gave me a pivot instead. And do you want to know what hit me as I was writing this book? I did find some balance in the pivots. These pivots showed me even more clearly what's most important in life. They showed me that it's okay to slow down and take care of myself or my family and friends in need. They showed me that I could get knocked down... but get back up again on my own timeline.

> What I've discovered is that pivots and shifts don't mean I'm failing; they mean He's redirecting me. And He's been slowly showing me the purpose behind these pivots this year. When something like this happens in life, the key is not to doubt yourself in the detours, but to trust that He's working, even when it feels like everything's shifting beneath your feet.

I tell you all of this not for you to feel sorry for me. I know how blessed I am, and that there could be so many worse things going on in my life. Instead, I am telling you this because it's real life. This is my story. It's had its ups and downs and will continue to, no doubt.

Through the struggles of this year, I've had moments of doubt creep back in, wondering if I'm still in the right place doing the right thing. I've had to turn to prayer and reflection to make me realize that yes, indeed, I am. One way I know that God is being intentional at this time in my life is this book that I'm writing at this moment.

It was laid on my heart years ago to write a book, and the idea behind what the book would be about came to me a couple of years ago, but I sat on it... until this year. The year of the pivots. The year when I have struggled more emotionally, physically, and mentally than I had from 2017 to 2019. That's when I heard Him telling me: the time is now.

It seemed crazy at first, but I felt such a strong pull to do just that.

Anthony knew this dream of mine, and when I told him I thought it was the time, you guessed it, he said, "Let's do this." He will never not support me, my timing, or my dreams. When I told my team that this was the year I was going to make writing this book happen, they were all in, too. They all agreed that it would be good for me to get some of this out of my brain and onto paper.

I'll never forget telling my parents and my sister and their excitement for me. My mom has been telling me for years, "Stacey Michelle, you need to write a book." She was planting that seed all those years ago because she knew I was capable of doing it. My dad will probably be the first one to buy a copy (and maybe even buy twenty of them), and my sister will be shouting it from the rooftops, showing everyone what I've done.

Thank you to my sweet family for that support and belief in me.

Once I knew I had the support of my family and my team to help get me through this chapter, the stars started to align. Through connections I've built over the years with other business owners, I found a book publisher and signed on. It became real; it was happening. We had a timeline, and I was finally doing this. I started the buildup on the page of the biggest super-secret spy project yet, and it was so fun to see the guesses.

I went to my parents' lakehouse to spend a couple of days writing and getting started on the book, and when I tell you it was one of the most therapeutic times in my life, I mean it. I sat there on the deck, looking at the beautiful blue lake, my happy place, and started all the way back at the beginning of my journey, and I began to write. My hands couldn't type as fast as the thoughts in my brain, and it came pouring out of me. God was bringing me right back to my why and telling me, "This is where you are supposed to be, so do not doubt."

So I wrote. And that night, the most beautiful sunset occurred, and if you know me at all, you know I love a sunset. I sat on that deck and cried. Every emotion I had inside of me since 2013 came pouring out. The good, the bad, and the ugly, but mostly the grateful. I had built something amazing, something that my family is proud of, something that God called me to do, something that a community of thousands and thousands of ladies relies on. And I was soon going to become a published author. Just… wow.

It all became so clear in that moment that the timing of writing this book was perfect because God needed me to remember every moment of this story… right now.

The next day, I was able to go Live and finally share the secret. And of course, the reaction was priceless and amazing. The excitement was real, and we began collecting stories from the community, many of which were featured in this book.

To everyone who submitted a story, even if it didn't get featured, I want you to know that I read them all. Each and every one was so heartfelt and so kind, and each and every one left an impact on my life, just like I hope I leave on yours. Each time I've sat down to write since those days at the lake, it has just felt right. It's beyond therapeutic, and it's kept me grounded and centered during such a crazy year.

God has reminded me that just because it gets hard doesn't mean it's time to give up. It might actually mean I'm exactly where I'm supposed to be, or that maybe I'm on the verge of a breakthrough I don't see coming.

> Obedience doesn't guarantee ease, but it does guarantee His presence. And sometimes, the biggest confirmation of your calling comes in the seasons that test you the most.

On the days when things felt hard and heavy, I kept showing up. On days when I needed to be lifted up, my community lifted me up, without even knowing what they were doing. As much as I hear from them what I mean to them and how I help them, I hope they know they helped me tenfold, in more ways than they will ever know.

God, family, friends, Wilshire, and travel, those are some of the things in life that matter to me the most.

I know many of you have pivots in your life too. You have unexpected twists, hard chapters, moments that knock the breath out of you, and seasons where everything changes when you aren't ready. But just like me, those pivots in your life are not random. They're not wasted, and they're not the end.

There's purpose in what you've walked through, even the parts you wish you could skip. If you're in a high season, God's guiding you. If you're in a low season, God is holding you.

And if you're somewhere in between, trying to figure out which way is up, He's with you there, too. Your pivots are shaping you, strengthening you, and preparing you, even when you can't see it yet. As you think through your own life, I bet you can see those pivot moments too.

The times everything changed, the moments that stretched you, the unexpected adjustments you didn't want but needed. Maybe you're in one now. Maybe you've been in one for a long time. Maybe you're coming out of one with a new perspective. Wherever you are, hear me when I say this: you're not off track. You're not behind. And you are not forgotten.

> God works through every pivot, yours and mine, to realign us with our purpose.

So keep going, keep trusting, keep showing up in the highs, the lows, and all the middle spaces in between, because there's purpose in your pivots too. Kandy D. has had to face so many challenges and pivots lately, and I wanted to share her story with you.

―――――

KANDY D.'S STORY

I had been following some online crafters for a while, and one day Wilshire Collections popped up as a suggested page to follow on Facebook. Looking back now, I'm blown away by the impact that was made in my life by clicking that little follow button.

Stacey became my go-to when I needed an escape from the daily madness. I found her to be easy to relate to, down-to-earth, and engaging. Watching her videos was like hanging out with a friend.

I joined the Printable Club in the DC and was all in. The next year, Stacey announced the DC Getaway. Just twenty tickets for an opportunity to meet Stacey in person, craft shop, and eat in Tennessee.

I wanted to go so bad, but I had never done anything like this before. I went back and forth, and as I watched the number of available tickets dwindle, it was finally down to one remaining ticket, and my heart screamed, "Do it." And boy, am I glad I did.

Twenty strangers met that fateful day in November. We did crafts, ate an amazing lunch, and went shopping. But the best part was that twenty strangers were forming the bonds of friendship.

My beautiful DC Getaway girls have become such an important part of my life. Now, three years later, we still keep in touch almost every day. We have supported each other through tough times. We've prayed for one another and celebrated some big moments in life with each other. And we've had a chance to reunite at two more Wilshire Live events.

The power of what I like to call the Wilshire Effect has affected me the most profoundly this year. On December 31, 2024, a pivot happened that I didn't see coming. I was diagnosed with stage four rectal cancer and started chemotherapy infusions in January 2025. The Getaway girls flooded me with love, prayers, and support, and it was such an amazing feeling.

I knew that I would be receiving infusions through June, and then I would start radiation. But in November of 2024, I had bought my ticket for Wilshire Live 2025, which was in April, and I needed to go now more than ever. In February, I got really sick, ended up having emergency colostomy surgery, and spent a week in the hospital.

Wilshire Live was now only about eight weeks away, and I just couldn't see how it would be possible. Over the next few weeks, I started to regain my strength. My infusions were going well, and I wasn't suffering from too many side effects.

In late March, I asked my oncologist if he thought it would be okay for me to travel to Tennessee for the live event, and he gave me a resounding yes. The affirmation that he felt I could do it empowered me to work as hard as possible to make sure I was strong enough. Our plans were set, the Airbnb was booked, and my husband and I were driving down to Tennessee.

I couldn't have been more excited, but I was also scared. Could I manage the pain and fatigue? Would I have enough stamina to get through the day of activities?

I really wasn't sure. The day finally came to travel. The drive went well, and we arrived in Tennessee on Wednesday evening.

I was standing in line the next day before the doors opened, and you could just feel the energy. We were peeking in the windows, checking out the setup, and watching the Wilshire team buzz around, handling all the little details. Then the doors opened, and as we poured in, the smiles, the hugs, and the laughter were a salve for my soul.

There's an electricity that fills the room at a Wilshire Live event. It's hard to explain in words. After an amazing meal, fun shopping, and time spent connecting with friends, Olden knew I was exhausted, but in the best way possible.

For the first time in months, cancer wasn't all I could think about. My heart was happy, and my brain was stimulated. I slept well that night.

The live event the next day was amazing. You could just tell how much of themselves Stacey and her team poured into every detail. Each component had meaning.

I almost felt like I was floating throughout the day, like I was being lifted up and carried by the amazing energy in the room. The Wilshire Effect was in full force. I came home from Wilshire to live so happily.

My cup was full, and I was ready to continue my fight with cancer. Even though I'm still fighting, I found that it's really important that you continue to live your life as normally as possible. I want to add in here, she just told me today that as of today, there's no evidence of disease.

Stacey and the connections I've made through Wilshire have been medicine to my heart and soul, and I can't wait to attend Wilshire Live 2026 cancer-free.

———

Kandy is a true example of faith during the pivots. And recently she shared with me that they have now found no evidence of disease… God is good!

I would be lying if I told you that I wasn't nervous about writing this chapter. I knew this story had to be shared, but writing about the past was easier for me than writing about the current. The year of the pivots is still happening as I write this. I'm still dealing with things, walking this path, and figuring things out. It feels so real and raw to write about. But it also feels right to share this side of things and to be transparent.

I have found purpose in my pivots. I've found so many blessings among the pivots, and I have no doubt this year has made me stronger.

Pivots are so much deeper than we might think at times.

A few things I've learned along the way through all of them: faith over fear, real over perfection, and obedience over control.

Control is a hard one for me. I've had to learn to let go of so much over the years, but it never seems to come easily. The truth is, I'm a planner by nature. I've always been the type who wants to know the plan, the timing, the outcome, and the next step. I like tidy answers and clear pathways. I like knowing that if I work hard enough, I can fix it, prevent it, or make it happen.

But God doesn't work like that. And honestly, thank goodness He doesn't, because in every season of my life, the health struggles, the business pivots, the scary decisions, and the moments I stepped out before I felt ready, He has gently reminded me over and over again, "Stacey, I'm in control, not you."

Letting go has looked different in every chapter of this journey. Letting go of needing things to be perfect before I go Live. Letting go of knowing how it will all work out when I take a leap. Letting go of the fear that something will go wrong. Letting go of feeling like I have to do everything myself for it to be done right. Letting go of the idea that I can keep hard things from happening if I just plan harder.

Spoiler alert: I can't.

Every time I loosen my grip, God tightens His. Every time I finally release the thing I've been clinging to, He shows me He had a better plan the entire time.

Control is rooted in fear.

Obedience is rooted in trust.

And God keeps calling me back to trust.

Trust that He knows the bigger picture.

Trust that He's not surprised by anything that blindsides me.

Trust that He can multiply what I surrender.

That's exactly what 2025 was about for me, not just the pivots, but the trust that had to come alongside those pivots. Because here's the thing: every pivot has a purpose. Even the ones I didn't want, didn't expect, or didn't understand at the moment, God doesn't waste a single redirection.

Every time He closes a door, shifts my path, or nudges me somewhere new, it's always leading me closer to the place He meant for me to go all along. I began to realize that the pivots of this year weren't meant to break me. They were meant to build me, to refine my purpose, to strengthen my faith, and to prepare me for what God was calling me into next, whatever that may be.

Looking back at all the pivots, the ups, the downs, the *Oh my Lanta what's happening?!* moments, I can see now that every single one was leading me somewhere.

Not by accident. Not by luck. But by a God who cares about every detail of my life, even the messy ones.

These pivots tried to derail me at times, but instead, they helped define me.

They taught me to trust God more than my own plans. They show me that purpose grows in the places where certainty doesn't exist.

And here's what I now know with confidence: if I'm still breathing, He's still building. If the page hasn't turned, it's because the next chapter is going to matter. And as much as I've grown and changed through all of this, I know one thing for sure: my story isn't finished.

The next chapter is all about the One who's been holding the pen the entire time and the One who reminds me daily that this is bigger.

CHAPTER 12
GOD IS IN THIS STORY

I hope you've seen God and His goodness woven through every single page of this book. He's been the thread holding it together from the start. I hope you realize that my story isn't over, and neither is yours.

One of my favorite songs is "God Is In This Story" by Katy Nichole and Big Daddy Weave. I've blasted it on repeat during some of my hardest days and on some of my most grateful ones.

And every time it plays, I'm reminded it's true. He's in every inch of my story, and He's in every inch of yours, too. All those years ago, I stepped out in faith with nothing more than a paintbrush and a dream.

I thought I knew what I was building, but what God was painting behind the scenes was so much bigger than I could have ever imagined. With every decision I made, every do-it-scared moment, every triumph and every heartbreak, and every pivot, He was there. Guiding, protecting, redirecting, strengthening, whispering, "Keep going. I'm not done yet."

We have to give our battles over to Him and let Him fight them for us. Let Him lead our story. This story from Alice Anne U. is a great example of just that.

———

ALICE ANNE U.'S STORY

Before the 2025 live event, I was diagnosed with endometrial cancer.

Going to the live event, I felt a big dark cloud over me and even thought about not attending. My husband encouraged me that I would feel better going. We prayed in the car before I got out at the venue to get in line.

I didn't know anyone there, and I was coming alone. Two ladies in front of me in the line were smiling at me before I even got there. We exchanged names and became fast friends and sat together the entire weekend.

We did an activity when Stacey played "This is How I Fight My Battles," and we put our notes in a basket about what we wanted to let go of and hand over to God.

I wrote that I would give God my battle of my surgery in the coming weeks to release my fear. I shared with Stacey and Kellie to please be my prayer warriors, as they too had both recently had surgery. God not only answered my prayers, but I'm cancer-free.

I'm so thankful for this group and how God used Stacey in our connections. Stacey has been a true light by being a woman of faith, and support is a true reflection of her faith. I've said so many times that when I grow up, I want to be just like her. I love this community and the friendships that will stick together.

I love how God shows up in our group and these events and is part of this story.

———

And friend, I want you to hear this clearly: God is in your story too, not just the highlight reel, not just the pretty parts, and not just the chapter that feels easy or makes sense.

He's in the mess, he's in doubt, he's in the pivots, he's in the waiting, and he's in the parts that you don't talk about. He's in the places where you feel unqualified, unseen, or unsure. Every single day, he's writing something beautiful in you, even when you can't see the full picture yet.

So let me ask you: where is he nudging you? Where is he calling you to create, to connect, to forgive, to grow, to step out in faith, to start something new, or to let something go? Because if there's anything my journey has taught me, it's this:

> God will meet you exactly where you are, but he loves you too much to just leave you there.

He has a purpose for you, a plan for you, a story for you that's still unfolding in ways you can't imagine yet. The same God who took an ordinary girl with a heart for decorating and turned it into this beautiful, joy-filled, life-changing community is the same God who's holding the pen to your story, too. And friend, he's just getting started.

How amazing is that? Beyond all that God has done, I hope you have seen in this book that this community is the heartbeat of Wilshire. It's going to be hard to put into words what this community means to me, and I don't think I'll ever be able to thank you enough for how much you have blessed my life, but I'm sure going to try.

To the Wilshire community: wow, where do I even begin? Every time one of you sends me a message or leaves a comment telling me how I've helped you, encouraged you, or brought joy into your life, I find myself thinking the same thing: *You have helped me a thousand times more.*

Truly, the impact this community has had on my own life and on the life of my family is something I will never be able to fully put into words. You've walked with me through my highest highs and my lowest lows. You've cheered me on, prayed for me, laughed with me, lifted me up, and believed in me, even on days when I struggled to believe in myself.

From the very beginning, you accepted me exactly as I was: messy and imperfect, real, emotional, creative, passionate, anxious, excited, all of it. You never asked me to be anything other than Stacey. You've embraced me, trusted me, and shown me a level of kindness and loyalty that still stops me in my tracks.

Y'all know I call you *my ladies*, and it's because you truly live in my mind and my heart every single day. When I create, I think, *What would my ladies love?* When I design something new, I think, *What would make the ladies' lives and homes cuter?* When I make a decision, big or small, I think, *How will this serve my ladies?* At night, you're on my mind. In the morning, there you are again.

You're woven into every part of my purpose. Wilshire is not just a business for me; it's a calling. And you are the reason I pour my whole heart into every printable, every pillow cover, every craft, every Live, every event, every late-night brainstorming session, and every prayer that's been prayed over this business. All of it.

You've shared your lives with me. You've allowed me to enter your homes. You've embraced my family. You've donated to causes close to my heart. You've shown up for me and for one another. And because of that, you've shaped me into the woman I am today.

I honestly cannot imagine my life without you or Wilshire. When I look back at the girl in 2013 with that paintbrush and a dream, I can see now how God was already preparing my heart for all of this. But even then, I never could have dreamed of *this*: a community so kind, so thoughtful, so supportive, and so filled with love and joy and sincerity.

You are everything I didn't even know to pray for. You are the blessing I didn't see coming. You are proof that God really does exceed our expectations.

I often find myself wondering: *Why me?* Why was I trusted with a community like this? Why was I given this platform?

Why do I get to wake up and live my passion with all of you by my side? And honestly, I don't know, but I don't have to know, because God does. I trust that He chose each of us to be here for a reason.

And that reason has unfolded in the most beautiful ways. Whatever His purpose is, I'm grateful for it. I'm humbled by it. And I'm forever changed because of you.

So to my ladies, my DC girls, my PC girls, my Pillow Besties, my Double Dippers, my Triple Dippers, and every single soul who has ever supported Wilshire in any way, thank you. Thank you for believing in me. Thank you for trusting me.

Thank you for welcoming me into your lives and your hearts. Thank you for showing me what real community looks like. *Thank you* will never be enough, but from the bottom of my heart, thank you for everything.

You are the heartbeat of this story, and you always will be.

With all my love,

Stacey

———

A few other people wanted to leave a special message to the community.

A MESSAGE FROM ANTHONY

To the Wilshire community: grateful. That is the best word to describe the way I feel about you all. I have been there since the beginning, and to see this community grow the way it has is just truly remarkable.

The love and support you have for Stacey will never go unnoticed or forgotten. I have had the pleasure to meet some of you through several live events, and I witnessed that love you have for Stacey and my family. It's truly something that can't be put into words.

I want to thank everyone for being part of this wonderful community and for the continued support you've shown Stacey over the years, because without you, this wouldn't be possible. Thank you doesn't seem to cover it, but I appreciate each and every one of you.

Anthony

———

NOW A MESSAGE FROM MY TEAM

To our incredible Wilshire community, if there's one thing every single one of us agrees on, it's this: you are truly something special. Each of us came onto Team Wilshire at different times in different ways with different backgrounds, but the impact this community has had on our lives is the same. You've changed us, you've blessed us, and you've shown us what kindness, joy, and genuine connection really look like.

We've all worked with different people, different companies, and different online spaces, but nothing, absolutely nothing, compares to the magic of this community. Whether we meet you in person in Nashville or connect with you from afar, the warmth you give is real and rare. Stacey has created a space on the internet that feels safe, positive, uplifting, and full of life, which allows you to show up for each other in ways that still amaze us, celebrating the highs, praying, encouraging, and lifting one another up like a true family.

Serving you isn't just a job for us, it's an honor and a blessing. We feel purpose in our days because of what Stacey has created and because of you. We work hard because you deserve nothing less.

And working alongside Stacey, watching her lead, love, create, and show up with honesty, humor, grace, and faith, that has been one of the greatest gifts of all. But what makes it even more special is seeing how you respond to her with loyalty, trust, compassion, and joy. It's proof of the beautiful connection that this community is built on.

So thank you for the love you pour out, the encouragement you offer, the smiles you bring, and the kindness you show to one another and to us. Thank you for making this a place we genuinely look forward to showing up for every single day. Some of us may only be behind the scenes, but please know we all feel your light, your love, and your joy.

And we are so grateful to be a part of this story with you.

Team Wilshire

———

I hope all of this makes you feel as special as you are.

To my team, the best is yet to come, and having you by my side means the world to me. I know we will show up in 2026 with the same love and loyalty for the business while keeping the community and mission statement in mind.

OUR MISSION STATEMENT

At Wilshire Collections, we are passionate about helping women learn to create, decorate, and find joy in their homes. Our mission is to encourage women to build confidence in their decorating and DIY skills by sharing tutorials, ideas, inspiration, and beautiful pieces for their homes. We strive to make women feel included as they are surrounded by a community of like-minded women filled with creativity, laughter, and learning. Every aspect of this journey is an opportunity to find joy and turn your homes into spaces that make you happy and proud!

We will focus on our core values of creativity, making a difference, authenticity, integrity, customer satisfaction, teamwork, community, and impact.

We will do big things together, and we will continue to grow, learn, and be challenged. And we will do it together. A thank-you will truly never be enough for all that each of you do!

As I'm sitting here, wrapping up writing this book, the new year is fast approaching.

I would be lying if I said I didn't wonder what that would mean or look like. I think it's normal to wonder and have a general curiosity about what's next. One of my favorite things about starting a new year is the unknown.

There are so many things that happen over any given year that you never knew were going to come. I love to hope, dream, and cast visions this time of year for the next year. And I'm always anxious to see how it will unfold.

As you will have gathered from earlier passages in the book, one thing I've done for years is pick a word of the year. I'm looking at my wall right now with the little signs I've made for my word each year. Some of them have been things like *"flourish," "believe," "thrive," "change," "focus," "intentional,"* and *"balance."*

When I was first writing this chapter, I didn't know what my 2026 word would be just yet. I've learned over the years that the right word always finds me when the time is right, usually after prayer, reflection, and a whole lot of *Okay, Lord, I'm listening.*

I've also learned that picking a word isn't about predicting your year. It's about preparing your heart for it. It's about surrender. It's about trust. It's about saying, "God, I don't know what this next chapter holds, but I know who holds me."

Right before this book went into the final editing stages, I prayed a big prayer one night before bed for God to give me a sign or reveal to me where He wants me next year and what my focus should be. I woke up early the next morning and shot straight up in bed with so much clarity: *Contentment!*

Contentment is what my heart was longing for.

I'm picking this word not because life is perfect and I'm always content, but because my soul is ready to rest in what *is and* be okay with what's not. I'm craving more peace, more quiet joy, more trust in the process. Less hustle, less stress, less pressure to do it all.

I want to slow down so I can breathe deeper. I want to find renewal in the everyday moments of life. I want to let go of so much worry. I want to do the work within myself that I've been putting off for far too long.

> To me, *contentment* is going to be about seeing the beauty right where I am, even in the waiting and even in the worry. It's going to be about choosing calm over chaos, trust over tension, and presence over pressure.

It's going to be about doing what I love most and loving on the community I've built, the most loyal of the loyal.

It's going to be about spending time with those who are most precious to me in life. It's going to be about being intentional with my time and my energy.

And honestly, it's a little bit scary. Because just like *balance*, which is so hard to achieve, I know living in a state of *contentment* won't come easy at times.

I know this word will guide me, stretch me, grow me, and remind me, just like every word before it, that *God is in this story*. Every year, every season, every next step. He already knows the path. He already knows the purpose. I just have to be willing to follow.

Here's what I do know going into the new year: this story isn't finished. And as you can see from this book, you're all a part of it now. As I close these pages, my prayer is simple: that you don't just see *my* story, or even the stories of this beautiful community, but that you see God's fingerprints all over them.

He's the author of it all: the connections, the healing, the laughter, the joy, the creativity, the courage, every bit of it. I'm beyond grateful He allowed me to be a small part of this much bigger story because this book isn't about what I've done. It's about what He's done and what He will continue to do in each of our lives if we lean in and let Him.

If God can take a girl with no real plan, just a paintbrush and a dream, and turn it into *this*, He can do the same with your story. So don't underestimate what He can do. I had my "this is bigger" moment back in 2018, the moment everything shifted when Missy sent me that message, and I've continued to have them ever since.

> God keeps showing me over and over that He writes stories far more beautiful than anything I could dream up on my own.

And my hope is that as you lay this book down, you'll feel a little nudge in your own heart, a little whisper that says, "Look around, pay attention: this is bigger than you think."

Look at the people He's placed in your life. Look at the blessings you didn't expect. Look at the hard moments that refined you. Look at the joy that surprised you. Look at the places where you can't deny His goodness, because, friend, He's working in your story too.

Even in the chapters that don't make sense yet. Even in the waiting. Even in the pivots. Even in the parts where you feel unqualified, unsure, or unseen, your story is not finished. Your purpose is not finished. Your *bigger* moment may just be right around the corner. I don't know what's next for me in life, in Wilshire, or in this community, but I know the One who does.

And that is what gives me peace. That's what gives me excitement for the future. That's what gives me confidence when the next chapter feels a little unknown, because the unknown isn't scary when you trust the One holding the pen.

So here's to the chapter still being written.

Here's to the women who've walked this journey with me.

Here's to the lives touched in ways I'll never fully understand.

Here's to the God who took something ordinary and made it extraordinary.

And here's to the beautiful truth that we get to live out together:

This is bigger. It's always been bigger. And He's not done yet.

CONCLUSION

As I close this book, I'm struck by how faithful God has been through every part of this journey. What started with a paintbrush and a whole lot of doing it scared has turned into a story only He could write.

A story filled with connection, creativity, laughter, healing, and a community that continues to amaze me every single day. And here's what I know now more than ever: this story is bigger than me, and it always has been. My prayer is that something in these pages reminds you that your story matters, too.

God is working in ways you can't even see yet. He is using your gifts, your struggles, your heart, your pivots, and your dreams to create something beautiful, something bigger than you imagined. I hope you also realize this community is powerful.

What we've built together is rare and special. You have allowed me into your homes, your hearts, and your stories. And in return, you've changed my life in ways I'll never fully be able to explain.

Thank you for laughing with me, praying with me, crafting with me, decorating with me, whisper-shopping with me, and walking through so many seasons together. You've shown me that God can take strangers on the internet and turn them into family. And the best part? We're just getting started.

There are chapters ahead that none of us can see yet, but I promise you this: God is in them already. While reading this, I hope you laughed, I hope you felt seen, I hope you felt encouraged, and most of all, I hope you felt God's presence in these pages. My greatest hope in writing this book was not that you would learn about *my* story, but that you would begin to see the beauty in *yours*: the purpose in your pivots, the strength in your struggles, the value in your voice, and the *"this is bigger"* picture.

If these pages encouraged you, inspired you, or reminded you that you're not alone, then every moment of writing them was worth it. Thank you for being part of my journey. Thank you for letting me be part of yours.

There's a moment from my life that I think about often, especially as I sit here finishing this book…

Years ago, when my grandmother, whom we called "Mere," was nearing the end of her life, our family gathered in her hospital room to say our goodbyes. As we all walked in, she looked up at us and said, "What an honor." Those words have stayed with me ever since.

Mere was so proud of everything I was doing in my life and my business, and even in her nineties, she was on FB watching and was blown away by this community. I have no doubt she's smiling down and proud. Especially right now.

I had a dream about her the other night, and I woke up with tears in my eyes. Because her words are exactly how this whole experience feels to me.

What an honor.

What an honor it has been to grow Wilshire Collections.

What an honor it has been to walk in my calling.

What an honor it has been to build this community.

What an honor it has been to have my family and faith at the center of it all.

I don't know what comes next, but I know it's going to be good, because He's in it. And because I get to walk into the future with all of you by my side.

So I'll carry Mere's words with me always… What an honor. What an honor this is, and always will be, bigger.

ACKNOWLEDGEMENTS

There are so many who have helped me and supported me in my journey, from the start of my business all the way up to writing this book and beyond. I am so thankful for every person I've crossed paths with and made connections with, as you are each a part of this bigger story.

To **Anthony**, thank you for being a constant source of love and support. You never questioned my dreams or made me feel like they were too big to achieve. That, plus your constant help with the boys, the house, and everything in between, is one of the main reasons I've been able to achieve so much. You are my rock, my soulmate, the best dad, and my best friend, and I'm so thankful we get to walk this life together. I wouldn't want it any other way!

To **my boys**, being your mom is the greatest blessing of my life, and you have been there for me every step of this process from the time you were little until now. I hope I have shown you that no dream is too big to chase and that you can do anything if you work hard and put your mind to it. Thank you for being protective of me, for making me laugh, and for embracing the craziness that a public online job can bring to a family. You both make me proud every single day.

To **my mom and dad**, thank you for raising me to be resilient and hardworking and for embracing my creativity from a young age so that I could let that part of me flourish. I know I get a lot of my work ethic from you, Dad, as you were always so hardworking and dedicated. And Mom, your eye and talent for decorating were passed right down to me, and that gift and talent have changed my life. I'll never be able to thank you enough for your love and support for me in both life and business.

To **my sister Blair**, this business started with you by my side, and while on paper you may not be part of it now, you have been and always will be part of this story. I know you are one of my biggest cheerleaders, and I love that we get to do life together in both raising our boys and growing businesses alongside each other. I couldn't imagine life without you by my side. Thank you for believing in Wilshire way back then and continuing to believe in it now!

To **the Collins fam**, from the minute you welcomed me into your family (and even before), you have loved me unconditionally like I'm your own. You'll never know what that means to me. I'm so blessed to have each of you in my life. MIL and FIL, we can't forget the fact that you raised an amazing son who supports me in all I do, and that is something that you should be so proud of!

To **my grandmother Mere**, I know you are smiling down right now and saying, "Stacey Michelle, I'm just so proud of you." Even in your nineties, you were on Facebook, watching my videos and beaming with pride when you would tell me something you saw on my "channel." I think of you so often and how amazed you were by all I was doing. I hope I continue to make you proud in all the days and years ahead.

To **the dream team,** you all came on at different times, but it feels like we've all been together forever. Each of you is so special to me and plays such a crucial role in my life and in Wilshire. We aren't meant to walk these kinds of things alone, and so much of what I do couldn't be done without you by my side. Thank you will never quite be enough for the appreciation I have for each of you! You are what helps make Wilshire what it is today, along with all the others previously mentioned who help me in my business in various ways behind the scenes. Thank you for all you do to support this business of mine!

To **Sarah and the Elevate Mastermind girls**, it's been an amazing few years being together, learning from Sarah, and growing together. I could not and would not want to do any of this without people just like all of you by my side. You've been there for me through so many new adventures, the highs, the lows, and everything in between. Rising tides lift all ships, and I'm so thankful to be riding the waves of business and life with each of you!

Thanks **to the ones who believed in me and helped me** early on. Stacey H. became one of my first biz buddies and supported me tremendously. Brooke R. took a chance on me with that Facebook Live way back in the day and has been there for me every step of the way since. Vanessa C. and Danielle S. are always there for me, no matter how much time passes. Cara P. and Angie J. stepped up to help me in my garage, with events, and so much more. And friends like Kristan, Jen, Carrie, and Christine let me use their garages for shipping, helped pack up boxes, worked my events, and more.

I can't thank you all enough!

To **my Alpha Gam college besties**, you all have known me since way before Wilshire, and I love that you have been part of my life for all of it. You each make it so clear how proud you are of all I'm doing, and I truly can't tell you what that means to me. Our annual trips mean so much to me, and these kinds of friendships are a true treasure and blessing!

To **my local friends**: you know who you are, the ones on the endless and ongoing text thread! Thank you for all of your love and support, and most importantly, your friendship and the laughter you've given me over the years! We are the farthest thing from a group of "fun busters," and I'm so blessed to have each of you in my life!

To **all the other biz coaches and biz friends** I have made along the way through coaching groups, masterminds, and more: each of you is so special to me. There are simply too many to name, but I know you know who you are if you are reading this. I can't imagine doing life without you! It takes a village, and thank you for being part of mine!

And of course, **thank you to God** for being the One who holds the pen. The One who has taught me more than anyone and stretched me farther than I ever thought possible. You are the reason I've been able to do any of this, and I will forever sing your praises and give you all the glory! Thank you for making me realize all those years ago that this was bigger so that I could live out my calling in life!

ABOUT THE AUTHOR

Stacey Collins is the owner and heart behind Wilshire Collections, a decorating, DIY, printable, and pillow-lovin' community that has grown far beyond anything she could have imagined when she first picked up a paintbrush back in 2013. A Southern-born-and-raised girl living just south of Nashville, TN, Stacey has always had creativity in her soul. As a child, if she wasn't directing a homemade "play," she was crafting, painting, or sporting one of her puff-painted DIY shirts. Her mom's deep love for design and decor shaped her early years, filling her childhood with seasonal decorating, bargain hunting, and endless inspiration. The name Wilshire comes from the street she grew up on, Wilshire Way, which is a reminder that sometimes the beginnings of your story show up long before you realize it.

Today, Stacey spends her days designing printables and pillows, creating decorating tutorials, whisper-shopping through stores, and crafting alongside a community of women who have become like family. She is passionate about helping women find confidence, creativity, and *joy* in their homes, not by spending a fortune, but by embracing inspiration, small tweaks, and meaningful touches that make a home feel like *you*.

She has been married to her husband, Anthony, for twenty-three years; he is her steady encourager, behind-the-scenes helper, and her constant source of love and support. Together they have two boys, Parker and Tyler, who are the greatest joys of their lives and the reason Stacey works so hard to create a balance between building her business and being fully present at home.

For the past fourteen years, Stacey has built Wilshire Collections from a paint-splattered garage dream into a thriving online community that includes the Decorating & Creating Community, the Printable Club, and the Pillow Cover Club. She's built a team of ladies who work alongside her to be able to love on and support the community and help her with all of her business needs. She's been featured in *Better Homes and Gardens, Good Housekeeping, Forbes Home, The Pioneer Woman*, and more.

Through each pivot, each challenge, each do-it-scared moment, and each leap of faith, she's discovered that her business was never really about crafts or decor; it was about connection. About joy. About purpose. About women supporting women. And ultimately, about God weaving something much bigger than she ever expected.

Her book is a reflection of that journey. It comprises a mix of her story, the stories of the women who have been impacted along the way, and the beautiful reminder that God is in every chapter, even the ones we don't understand yet.

Stacey's hope is simple: that her story inspires you to find your purpose, embrace your creativity, do it scared, and recognize the "bigger" moments God is writing in your own life. Because while she may have built a business… **It's the community that built the heart of it.**

So whether you're here for decorating ideas, crafting inspiration, a cute printable, an adorable pillow, or simply a dose of joy, Stacey is grateful you're part of this journey.

Because in her words, "All of you are my why!"

THANK YOU FOR READING MY BOOK!

Just to say thanks for buying and reading my book, I would like to give you a free printable + some other fun ideas and inspiration + share ways you can get connected with the Wilshire Community!

Stacey

Scan the QR code now to get yours:

I appreciate your interest in my book and value your feedback, as it helps me improve future versions. I would appreciate it if you could leave your invaluable review on my website and/or Amazon.com with your feedback. Thank you!

www.ingramcontent.com/pod-product-compliance
Lightning Source LLC
Chambersburg PA
CBHW051346280526
45784CB00007B/2834